BIG BEAD
JEWELRY

BIG BEAD JEWELRY

35 beautiful easy-to-make projects

Deborah Schneebeli-Morrell

NORTH LIGHT BOOKS

Dedication

To Zabiullah Noori who inspired me with his spectacular collection of semi-precious stones, and to his lovely family for their kindness and hospitality.

Distributed to the trade and art markets in North America by
North Light Books
An imprint of F + W Publications, Inc.
4700 East Galbraith Road
Cincinnati, OH 45236

ISBN 978-1-58180-896-4

First published in the United Kingdom in 2006 by Cico Books
An imprint of Ryland, Peters and Small
20–21 Jockey's Fields
London WC1R 4BW

Designed by Janet James
Edited by Gillian Haslam
Styled photography by Gloria Nicol
Step-by-step photography by Heini Schneebeli
Projects on pages 67, 98, 101, 103 and 125
designed by Rachel Piper

Acknowledgments

I would like to thank my good friend Gloria Nicol for her advice and encouragement and for taking most of the lovely photographs in this book. I am grateful to my husband Heini Schneebeli for his skill in taking the essential step-by-step photographs. A big thank-you to my publisher Cindy Richards for persuading me to take this commission and lastly, as ever, so many thanks to my editor Gillian Haslam for her calm influence and her seamless editing.

Contents

Introduction

Jewelry specially designed to make a bold statement and a big impact through the use of large beads has never been more fashionable. Clothes stores, specialist shops, and even chain stores are all overflowing with the most extraordinary variety of big-bead jewelry. These are often mass-made, expensive, and can be of poor quality. This inspiring book provides you with the techniques and ideas to create your own enduring quality pieces to rival any shop-bought item.

Gathering ideas

Look around at what is commercially available, as good ideas for combining beads can be found this way. It is also worth browsing through fashion magazines as the more you see, the more you can develop your own ideas and style. Flea markets, antique markets, and retro stores are brilliant places to find inspiring strings of beads or necklaces at a low cost which you can dismantle and use the elements to redesign a unique piece of your own jewelry. Surprisingly, it can be less costly to do this rather than sourcing beads direct from a supplier. One important consideration when buying your beads is to make sure the central threading hole is large enough to take your chosen cord. Beads with really large holes are less common.

There are now so many bead shops and websites where you can browse for beads. The choice is quite unbelievable, with beads originating from all over the world. You can spend as little or as much as you can afford; either way, it is possible to create an original piece to a professional standard. The sensitive use of color, size, texture, and form in the mix of beads and stones and good design are the key elements in making a striking piece of jewelry. The projects in this book will introduce you to these concepts and techniques and enable you to make your own jewelry.

Jewelry makes a wonderful gift, and by making your own you can tailor your piece to suit the recipient – everyone loves to receive a hand-made present. Children in particular are fascinated by jewelry and a number of the simple projects in the book are particularly suitable to make with children. Each project is graded and gives an estimated making time, so it will be easy to choose which projects to begin with.

From the sewing box

Some people are lucky enough to have inherited a sewing box or a box of buttons. These are often handed down from mother to daughter to grand-daughter and are treasured items, although very rarely are they used. During the days when most clothes were sewn at home, the button box would have been full of an array of different kinds of buttons. Shirt buttons in particular were always made from mother of pearl, and the larger examples are now collectors' pieces, but even rather more ordinary everyday buttons can be put to creative use.

It's not so long ago that so many crafts were practiced at home and people had skills handed down through generations. Making jewelry pieces from leftover scraps and buttons recreates some of that laudable self-sufficiency and gives you a real sense of continuing a celebrated tradition, as well as evoking a bygone era with a contemporary twist.

If you don't yourself have access to these inherited modest domestic objects, it is quite easy to find buttons and fabric in flea markets, junk shops, jumble sales, or charity shops. Several projects use old woollen blankets or sweaters that have been felted by simply washing them on a very hot cycle in the washing machine.

The skill in creating unique jewelry from mixed materials lies in the choice of color and texture combinations, as well as in the simple and original techniques. It is increasingly fashionable to combine old and new materials with combinations of textiles and beads. Try chunky wooden

beads with the felted wool or tiny clear seed beads with the mother-of-pearl shirt buttons.

By rolling two pieces of contrasting felted wool together you can make unusual fabric beads, or use embroidery wool tassels in combination with wooden beads threaded onto satin cord to make a striking necklace. Once you begin to work using these fabric, button, and bead combinations, you will find new ideas emerging and hopefully will go on to devise original projects of your own.

Treasures from the earth

Nothing can match the beauty of semi-precious stones. They are not made, they are mined from the very earth beneath our feet, and possess the most magical qualities of color, reflecting different tones at different times of the day.

Much has been written about the mythical properties of these lovely stones, and many people believe in the innate healing, protective, and energizing qualities they possess. It is not surprising that humans have bestowed these useful properties upon the stones over the centuries and today there is a definite resurgence of these ancient beliefs. This renewed interest, of course, leads to them being so much more readily available.

Even before you touch, see, or feel them, the names are so evocative and poetic. Lapis lazuli, lemon jade, turquoise, amazonite, rose quartz, moonstone, agate, amethyst, and serpentine – these are only a few of the extensive list of possibilities conveniently available today.

There are so many stones to choose from that it is entirely possible to find yourself quite carried away in a crystal shop. You will want to know more – where in the world are they mined, how common are they, how can they be used, what are their special properties?

Many bead suppliers and shops sell semi-precious stones that have been fashioned into beads of all shapes and sizes and they are usually fairly inexpensive, the larger examples naturally being the most costly. However, they are well within the budget of most people and can be used to create

an exquisite piece of jewelry a fraction of the price of a similar piece in a shop.

The more complicated carved beads will cost a little more and rightly so, as they are often carved with great care by people living in the developing world. These are ancient skills and can often be seen matched to historic pieces in our great museums. Use them in combination with other materials – for example, lapis lazuli flowers look lovely combined with the solid Indian silver beads, and threading them on leather cord emphasizes the natural qualities they possess.

Combine and contrast large stones with small chips or polished beads with roughly cut examples. Color is as important here as with other materials, and if you are not experienced in this field, making many of the projects in this book will help develop a sensitivity to color, texture, and form that will be reflected in your home-made pieces. You will always need to thread these stones on a secure cord or wire as they may be heavy and they are precious.

The glory
of glass beads

Although there are innumerable good mail-order bead websites, do try to visit bead shops as they are the most inspiring places. It isn't until you see the perfect bead, amongst the choice of thousands that you can envisage the design of your project. Good bead shops are staffed by knowledgeable enthusiasts and usually many examples of made-up jewelry are on show as an inspiration and a guide to new customers and novice beaders.

Glass beads make up the biggest category of beads. They are known worldwide and throughout history. Many stunning examples are to be found on display in museums and tell us much about the technical and trading capabilities of past civilizations.

The variety of glass beads can be quite dazzling at times. Some are chunky, recycled glass, which looks like it has been worn by the tides in the sea, others are figured and highly decorated, in particular the millefiori beads, which are made in Italy, the home of exquisite glass bead-making for centuries. Some lovely and inspiring examples have a silver foil lining encased within the bead, bringing a reflective, shimmering quality to the glass. These are often shaped and come in a huge variety of sizes.

Tiny glass seed beads are often referred to as rocailles. They come in many colors, both transparent and matte as well as metallic, and are particularly effective when used in conjunction with larger and more decorated feature beads. For a beginner, it may be worth buying a bead collection (these often feature the less expensive Indian beads, which can be highly decorative).

Good-quality, hand-worked beads can be expensive. These are European in origin and cover a wide range of decorative techniques and may be described as lamp beads, Venetian, Bohemian, or hand-wound glass furnace beads.

Beads from the Far East are now flooding the market, increasing choice and reducing the cost of buying quantities.

Pearls, silver, and sparkle

Of all the beads available, none can really surpass the beauty and elegance of a single pearl. This has always been a classic style favorite and is currently enjoying a fashionable revival, making it very easy to access.

Cultured freshwater pearl strings, which are produced in the Far East, are available in a range of sizes, and as well as the natural color, a wide choice of subtly dyed tones can be found. Some may be quite irregular in shape and others elongated, but all these variations help to add interest and enhance the quality of pearly iridescence. Although a little more expensive than most beads, they are not beyond the pocket of most people, especially if you shop around. It is often possible to see them piled high in flea markets or antique markets at very reasonable prices.

The really feminine quality of these jewels lends them to subtle combinations with other materials and they work well with real silver and small beads of semi-precious stones. It is important not to overwhelm the quality of the pearls with bright and striking color, but rather to enhance the unique quality with gentle tones and textures, such as silver chain and organdie ribbon.

Other beads with pearl-like qualities are the disks cut from mother-of-pearl or abalone shell. These are often drilled with a central or off-center hole and look exquisite knotted onto pale silk thread or almost invisible nylon monofilament. One or two of the projects in the book use a complete shell – these often have drilled or natural holes

in which other pearls or complementary beads can be threaded. Although a little expensive to buy, they can be easily fashioned into a striking pendant.

Silver charms, often with an ethnic or peasant quality, are mostly made in and around the Indian subcontinent. Because they are made from real silver, they will usually be sold by the weight. These can look quite lovely as a feature pendant in themselves or combined with silver chain, ribbon, or freshwater pearls.

Tools and equipment

What is unique about the projects in this book is how few specialist tools are needed. Two pairs of jewelry-making pliers are essential—chain-nosed pliers for pressing crimp beads flat and round-nosed pliers for turning wire into small loops, for example to attach an end pin securely to a chain. No other specialist equipment is needed, but it will be useful to have an ordinary pair of scissors and a large sewing needle (also known as a chenille needle) for threading beading elastic. Probably the most useful item to have in your kit is a beading mat made from a synthetic material with a soft pile. Place your beads here so they are easy to see and they will not roll away.

Left: To make a varied collection of jewelry you will need a variety of cords, threads, wires, rat tail, leather, suede, beading elastic, tiger tail, nylon monofilament, and ribbons. Luckily most beading suppliers will have a comprehensive selection of these essential items.

Left: Jewelry findings come in a variety of metals, including silver, gold, plated metal, copper, and bronze. You will need a variety of clasps, jump rings, and split rings, calottes, crimp beads and tubes, end pins, and eye pins. Earring "fish" hooks have been used in this book, although you could easily substitute other forms of earring attachments for those without pierced ears. It is best to use sterling silver or copper chains, as a pure metal always looks better and is easier to work with.

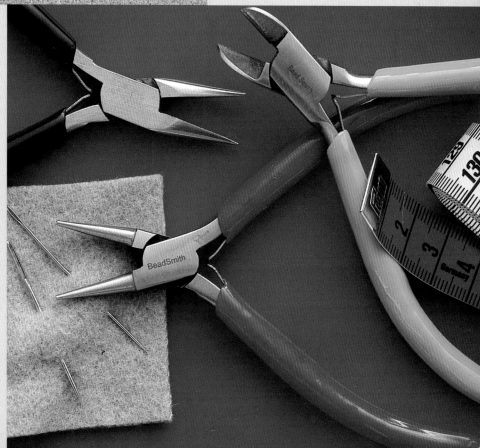

Right: You don't need many tools to make the projects in this book, Most essential are the round-nosed and chain-nosed pliers, wire cutters, a pair of scissors, a measuring tape, and a couple of needles with large eyes.

from the sewing box

The unusual combination of beads, buttons, and scrap fabric can be used to make stunning original jewelry. This chapter contains some of the simplest projects in the book and they will not take you long to make as they use materials that are easy to find. The intensity of color that you find in some fabrics, such as wool and felt, makes a striking feature when partnered with an assortment of wooden or glass beads. Once you start to feature buttons in your jewelry making, you will soon realize there are countless ways that they can be used. They are so adaptable and, as they already have holes drilled through, they are perfect for threading.

Right: Collect all kinds of scrap material for use in jewelry-making. Old blankets and sweaters felt easily if laundered on a hot wash, while embroidery thread – either wool, cotton, or silk – comes in an amazing array of colors.

Rainbow felted necklace

Technique:
WORKING WITH FELT AND FABRIC

Level of difficulty:
SIMPLE

Estimated making time:
1 HOUR

This richly colorful necklace is among the simplest projects in this book, and it is the skill in choosing the best combination of colors that makes it work so well. Wooden beads are easy to source, and you may even be able to re-use beads from a long-abandoned children's jewelry box. The felted wool squares are simply cut from old blankets or prettily colored sweaters which were destined for the charity shop.

you will need

Old woollen blankets or sweaters felted by washing on a hot wash (in blue, pink, terra cotta, and orange)

Needle with a large eye (also known as a chenille needle)

Beading elastic $1/32$in. (0.8mm) thick, approximately 32in. (80cm) long

16 bright pink wooden spacer beads

8 large oval wooden beads

Large silver-colored crimp bead

Scissors

Chain-nosed pliers

1. Cut out freehand 24 squares, approximately $3/4$in. (2cm) square, in each of the four colors of the felted wool.

2. Thread the needle with the elastic and start to push through the center of 12 pieces of felt in your first color.

TIP Save all sorts of fabric for this project, such as old patchwork pieces, worn blankets, or moth-eaten sweaters. You can always salvage enough from the original item for a really interesting project. Work with the colors you find, or you may like to dye fabric to match your beads. A really hot wash will easily felt any kind of wool (launder the woollen garment before cutting it into squares).

3. Follow with a pink spacer bead, a blue oval bead, and another pink spacer. Next, thread on 12 more pieces of felt in a different color. Repeat until you have used up all the beads and felt.

4. Thread the crimp bead onto one end of the elastic, pull to stretch it over your finger, and slide the other end through the bead. Pull firmly so that the necklace is tight with no elastic visible, then press the crimp closed with the pliers. Cut off the elastic ends and conceal the join inside one of the big beads.

To make a pretty matching bracelet, use the same technique as for the necklace but thread only four squares of felted wool between small flower-painted wooden beads.

Variation (*above*) This brilliantly colored necklace is created using the same simple technique of threading everything on beading elastic, but made to a longer length. This time the beads are interspersed with circles of frayed fabric in vibrant pink, pale lilac and soft green. Two styles of beads have been used here – circular orange wooden balls and flatter magenta-pink disks.

Woollen tassel necklace with wooden beads

This fun project is really very easy to make. Tassel decorations have become rather fashionable, and these are made from embroidery yarn, which is obtainable in a wide range of vibrant colors. The faceted purple wooden beads are interspersed with decorative dyed Indian seeds. The satin cord, or rat tail, is closed with a double knot and the loose ends are finished with brightly colored wooden beads. As long as the necklace fits over your head, use this method of closing to make the necklace any length you choose. This would be a particularly suitable project to make with children.

Technique:
KNOTTING OR TASSEL-MAKING

Level of difficulty:
SIMPLE

Estimated making time:
1¹/₂ HOURS

you will need

Embroidery yarn in a variety of colors, such as blue, pale green, light and dark pink, purple

5 large purple faceted beads

5 large decorative Indian seeds

12 selected smaller wooden beads

Rat tail – a thick length in deep purple and a thinner length in mauve

Scissors

Embroidery needle

1. To make the first tassel, wind the purple yarn four times around three fingers on your hand.

2. Remove the loop of yarn from your fingers and cut the loop from the ball of yarn. Thread a short length of a paler color around the purple threads and tie into a loop (this will be used to attached the tassel to the rat tail). Fold the yarn over and hold together, then tightly bind together ¹/₂in. (1cm) from the top using the same color yarn as the loop. Tie into a tight knot (the ends can be sewn in so that they are hidden). Make a total of 10 tassels in this way.

3. Lay out the two lengths of rat tail next to each other. Approximately 12in. (30cm) from one end, tie them together in a single knot. Thread the purple wooden bead onto the darker purple cord and then make another knot directly on the other side of the bead so that it is held firmly in place.

4. Thread a turquoise wooden bead onto the loop of the pale green tassel and thread the two rat tail cords through the remaining space. Tie another knot ³/₄in. (2cm) from the first purple bead, enclosing the tassel loop.

5. Continue threading and knotting in this manner, alternating the decorative seed beads with the large purple wooden beads until all the beads are used. Always tie a tassel in a knot between the larger beads. Add the last tassel and leave 12in. (30cm) of the rat tail free.

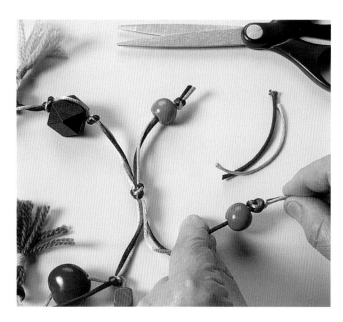

6. Tie a double knot in the rat tail to close the necklace, then thread a brightly colored bead onto each end about 4in. (10cm) away from the double knot. Tie a further knot after each bead to hold it in place.

Variation This necklace is made in the same way as the main project. The large dyed seed beads and glass beads are threaded onto a length of turquoise suede and woven cord. The tassels are made from embroidery floss and the smaller blue-toned beads are a mixture of glass, ceramic, and plastic.

Two-tone rolled felt bead bracelet

Technique:
ROLLING FELT INTO BEADS

Level of difficulty:
SIMPLE

Estimated making time:
1 HOUR

This funky little bracelet will inspire many other projects using similar techniques. As soon as you start experimenting with new materials, all sorts of new ideas suggest themselves to you. Instead of wooden beads to complement the felt, try using decorative glass beads for a more sophisticated look. The felted wool has been created by laundering old sweaters or blankets on a really hot cycle in the washing machine. This causes the wool to turn to felt.

you will need

Pieces of felted wool in green, orange, and pink

16 small wooden disks in pink, orange, red, and yellow

Thick beading elastic

Large crimp tube

Chain-nosed pliers

Needle

Chenille needle with a large eye

Strong thread

Scissors

Pins

Two-tone earrings
(*top right, opposite*) Use the single felt beads combined with wooden beads threaded onto brightly colored cord to make these amusing earrings.

1. Pin together double layers of the felt in different color combinations. Cut strips of the double layers measuring ³/₄in. (2cm) wide and 4³/₄in. (12cm) long. You need enough to make eight beads.

2. Tightly roll up the double strips, cutting off any spare felt if one overlaps the other. Sew a few tight stitches over the ends to hold the roll in place.

3. Thread the chenille needle with the beading elastic and push the needle through the area on the bead that has been stitched, making sure that it emerges on the other side of the bead centrally. Thread on two wooden beads and push the needle once more through another bead.

4. Continue threading in this manner until all eight felt beads are in place, separated by the colored wooden beads. Thread the crimp tube onto one end of the elastic and wrap it tightly around your finger—this stretches the elastic and allows you to thread the other end of the elastic through the crimp tube more easily. Pull the two ends and press the crimp tube firmly with the chain-nosed pliers to secure. Cut off the ends of the elastic.

Variation This more sophisticated bracelet uses monochrome shades of black, white, and gray for a striking effect.

Variation (*right*) Match different sorts of buttons and beads and make a variety of bracelets to wear together or to give away as original gifts. As shown here, this design works equally well as a fun multi-colored bracelet or as a sophisticated version with buttons in shades of ivory separated by pale blue beads.

Knotted cord button necklace

This button-box project uses the most run-of-the-mill buttons and demonstrates how everyday objects can be turned into something special. The buttons are used in blocks of the same color and threaded onto a knotted pale green cord which subtly complements the pinky-green selection of buttons. However, this uncomplicated necklace can look extremely stylish and looks particularly good set against a plain linen shirt. The cord is very much part of the design and is displayed at both ends where only single buttons are used between the knots.

Technique:
KNOTTING ON DOUBLE CORD

Level of difficulty:
SIMPLE

Estimated making time:
1¼ HOURS

you will need

2 yards (2m) pale green cord, approximately ¹⁄₁₆ in. (1mm) thick

Assortment of buttons of a similar size in colors such as pinks, mauves, and greens

A few slightly smaller buttons in similar colors, for the ends of the necklace

2 calottes for ending the cord

Split ring, ¹⁄₃ in. (7mm) in diameter

Flat snake clasp

Chain-nosed pliers

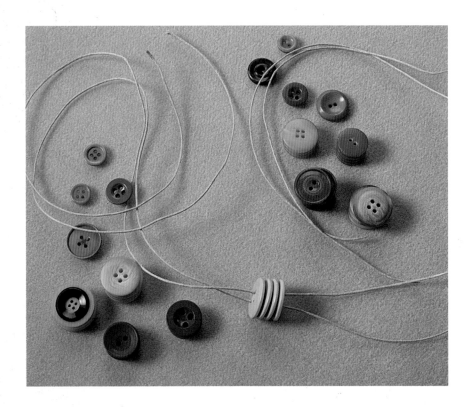

1. Sort your chosen buttons into piles of the same color – nine piles have been used here. Cut the cord into two even lengths. Thread the buttons which will appear in the center of the necklace onto the two cords, running each cord through different holes.

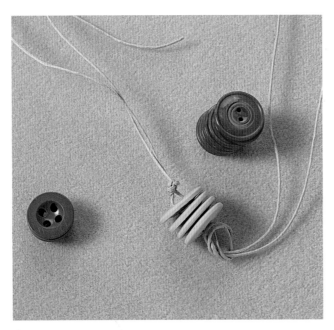

2. Tie the two cords together in a single knot on each side of the group of buttons. Make sure the buttons are in the center of the length of cord. Don't tie the cord too tightly – the buttons need to be a little flexible or the necklace will be too stiff.

3. Add more groups of buttons in the same way until they are all in place. Balance each side of the necklace. Leave slightly longer gaps between buttons toward the ends of the cord and add only single, smaller buttons between the knots at the end.

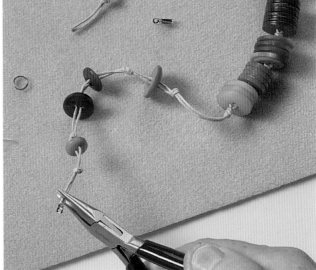

4. Make a final knot and cut the double cord 1in. (2.5cm) from the last knot. Place the cord ends into the calotte and bend over each side using the pliers. Press firmly to secure and repeat on the other end. Finally, attach the split ring onto one end and the snake clasp to the other.

Variation (*below*) These very ordinary brown and cream buttons appear far more interesting by interspersing them with amber beads saved from an old necklace. They have been threaded onto a leather cord and here the buttons run all the way to the end clasp.

Retro button bracelet

Technique:
THREADING CONTRASTING CORD

Level of difficulty:
SIMPLE

Estimated making time:
1 HOUR

These fantastic coat buttons are almost good enough to be in a museum. Made in the 1930s for ladies' coats, they display all the style and modernism of that period. The smaller buttons are of a similar date, all made from early plastic or Bakelite. The secret of the success of this project is the careful choice of color, the two tones of cord used, and the contrasting baby blue glass bead spacers, all of which add to the final effect. The bead and loop fastening is simple to make and can be applied to other projects.

you will need

4 large retro ladies' coat buttons

4 smaller buttons in a variety of colors, such as blue, brown, and white

24in. (60cm) length of natural leather cord, $^1/_{16}$ in. (1mm) thick

24in. (60cm) length of pink plastic cord, $^1/_{16}$ in. (1mm) thick

5 small pale blue glass beads with large holes

Scissors

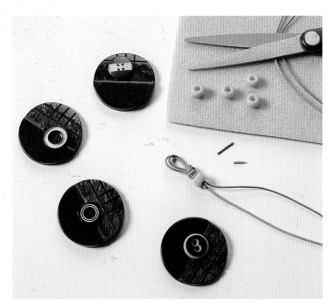

1. Lay your buttons out so that you can decide which button goes where. Thread the two cords through a blue bead and turn the end into a small loop, $^3/_4$ in. (2cm) long. Tie a knot and cut off the extra cord, leaving just enough to tuck into the blue bead.

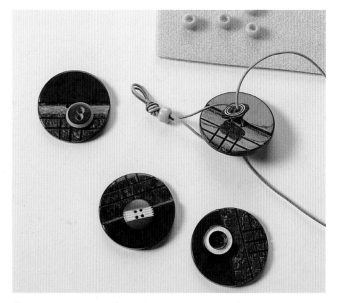

2. Thread the pink cord over and through the top button into the larger button beneath. Bring the leather cord through a separate hole from underneath the same button.

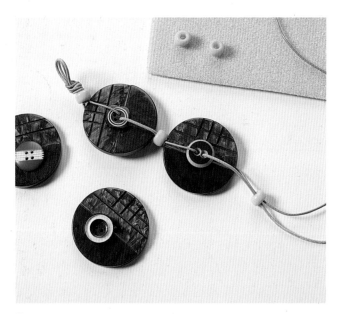

3. Push the cords together through a blue bead and thread the buttons as before. Continue in the same manner until all four sets of buttons are threaded.

4. Adjust all the buttons so that they fit firmly onto the two cords, then tie another knot at the opposite end to the loop tightly against the last button. Add the last blue bead and tie another knot ³/₄ in. (2cm) from the previous knot. Pull tightly and cut, leaving a "tail" of ¹/₈ in. (3mm). To fasten the bracelet, thread this bead through the loop at the other end of the bracelet.

Variation (*left and right*) If you are lucky enough to find a collection of interesting buttons, try making this striking necklace, which displays 1930s Bakelite buttons on two-tone leather cord. Scissors are the only tool required, and you won't need any jewelry findings to finish because the leather cord finishes in a sliding knot (see step 4 on page 56) and button clasp. Of course, you can make this project using thoroughly modern buttons if you wish — either way it will be a stunning piece that won't fail to be noticed.

Multi-strand earrings

Technique:
USING NYLON THREAD AND SEED BEADS

Level of difficulty:
FIDDLY

Estimated making time:
1 HOUR

These charming original earrings are simply made from three sizes of snow-white seed beads interspersed with mother-of-pearl shirt buttons. The pretty necklace shown here is made in exactly the same way. The three strands of differing sizes of beads are threaded onto the finest nylon thread and finished by threading all three strands through a single bead. They are secured with a crimp bead and covered by a calotte before fixing a ring clasp.

you will need

Nylon thread, 1/32 in. (0.5mm) thick

White glass seed beads in three different sizes

Selection of varied mother-of-pearl shirt buttons

6 silver-colored crimp beads

Silver fish-hook earring findings, or silver wire to make your own

Scissors

Chain-nosed pliers

TIP The earring findings have been made to fit the earrings so it was possible to thread two beads and a button in place above the attaching loop. It is not possible to do this when using ready-made earring hooks.

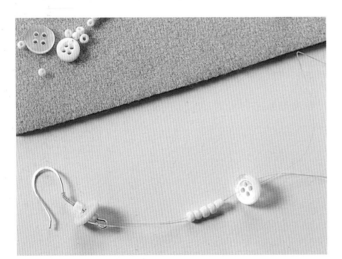

1. For each earring, cut three 12in. (30cm) lengths of nylon thread. Thread one length through the earring loop and fold in half. Thread five of the largest seed beads onto the double thread, add a button, passing both threads through one hole.

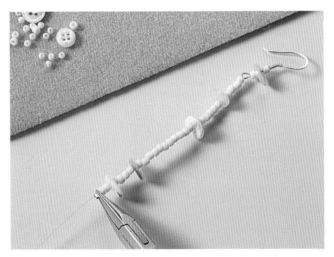

2. Add another six beads to the doubled thread, followed by another button. Continue in this manner, varying the number of beads between buttons until there are four buttons in place. Add another couple of seed beads and thread the nylon through the crimp bead. Press firmly with the chain-nosed pliers and cut off the excess. Thread two more lines of buttons and beads in the same manner. As you thread, lay the lines alongside each other so that you can vary the position of the buttons on each line. Finish each one with a crimp bead as before.

Pearl button earrings

Large mother-of-pearl buttons have been used here to create these beautiful, shimmering earrings. The large buttons were discovered in an inherited button box and the slightly smaller ones were bought from a haberdashery or notions store. The method of stringing them together is simple if a little fiddly, but you soon find that working with such lovely materials is a pleasure in itself. The trick is to thread them so the buttons lie flat and in line with each other.

Technique:
TWO-STRANDED THREADING WITH SEED BEADS

Level of difficulty:
SIMPLE BUT FIDDLY

Estimated making time:
UP TO 1 HOUR

you will need

Nylon monofilament thread, approximately 0.3mm thick

8 clear round beads $^1/_8$ in. (3mm) in diameter

10 small mother-of-pearl shirt buttons

2 large mother-of-pearl buttons, approximately $1^1/_4$ in. (3cm) in diameter

2 smaller mother-of-pearl buttons, approximately $^3/_4$ in. (2cm) in diameter

A small handful of the smallest clear seed beads you can find

2 silver earring fish hooks

2 silver crimp tubes, $^1/_8$ in. (3mm) in diameter

Chain-nosed pliers

Scissors

1. Cut a 12in. (30cm) length of the nylon monofilament and thread a single clear round bead centrally on it. Fold the nylon in half and thread each end through separate holes in a small shirt button.

2. Open out the two strands and thread each one with enough seed beads to reach the same hole on each side of the large button. Push the nylon thread through from each side and pull to tighten all the beads.

3. Thread each side again with enough seed beads to reach the top of the button, bring them together and thread through separate holes in the next shirt button. Follow this with a small round bead, followed by another shirt button.

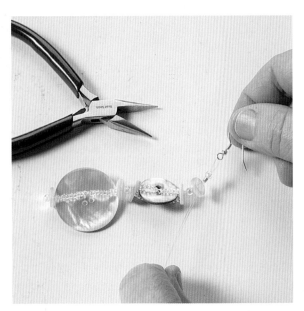

4. Repeat the same threading method, this time using the smaller pearl button. When you have reached the top, thread on a shirt button, then a round bead, then another shirt button. Next, add a crimp tube, followed by a final round bead. Thread the nylon through the loop at the base of the earring hook, then back through the last bead and crimp tube. Pull tightly and press the crimp tube firmly with the pliers to secure. Cut off the excess nylon. Repeat the steps for the second earring.

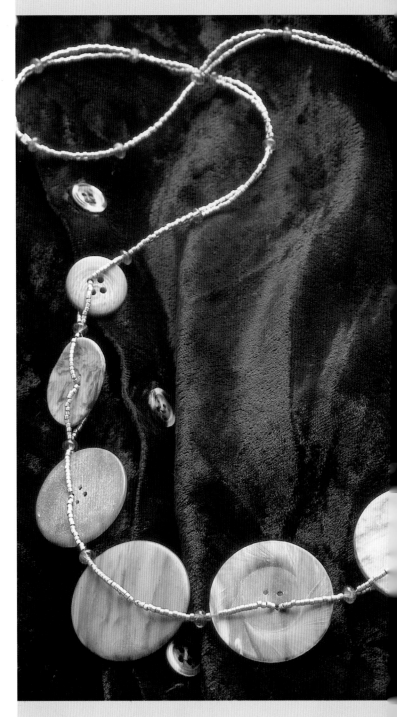

Variation (*above*) This necklace is made in a similar way but using a different colorscheme. The matte browns of the rather ordinary buttons are cleverly set off against the threading of glittering mauve delica beads spaced with small round amethyst beads.

Variation (*below*) This stunning necklace is a wonderful way of showing off beautiful old mother-of-pearl buttons. It has been strung in a similar way to the earrings, omitting the shirt buttons and just bringing the two strands together between the buttons with a single clear round bead. Make the necklace long enough to go over your head so that a clasp is not required. The two strands from either side are brought together and secured with a crimp tube.

CHAPTER 2

Treasures from the earth

It is a joy to work with the natural beauty of semi-precious stones – the variety of color is astonishing and each type of stone has its own particular feel, making it perfect to wear against your skin in the form of a necklace. These stones are widely available and relatively inexpensive, allowing you to make a piece of a jewelry to a professional standard but at a fraction of the retail cost. You can find raw uncut stones, polished bead shapes, and even complicated carved pieces. When using semi-precious stones, don't clutter them with a combination of beads or complicated threading. It is best to let them display their natural simplicity. To keep the natural theme and sympathy for the materials you are working with, use a pure metal for the clasps and findings.

Right: Semi-precious stones are very fashionable, but are not as expensive to buy as you might think. It is very rewarding to work with them, especially once you begin to learn about them and feel and see the different qualities of each stone.

Three-strand turquoise necklace with feature beads

The oval faux turquoise beads in this project come from China where they are experts at imitating semi-precious stones. When buying beads, to the unskilled eye it is easy to be confused – you may think you have bought the real thing but you may later discover you have purchased a brilliant fake instead. Here the brilliant turquoise color of the large oval beads has a wonderfully rich tone which, when combined with the old green glass beads and the genuine turquoise chips, makes this a pleasing piece of jewelry. The skill and interest in this piece is that it uses three strands, thus enabling different forms of threading.

Technique:
THREADING ON MULTIPLE THREADS

Level of difficulty:
FIDDLY BUT SIMPLE

Estimated making time:
1¼ HOURS

you will need

5 oval faux turquoise beads, 1in. (2.5cm) long

20 glass beads, 12 measuring ¼in. (5mm) and 8 measuring ³⁄₈in. (8mm) in diameter

Small turquoise chips, approximately 174 pieces needed in total

2 yards (2m) lengths of tiger tail, size 0.31mm

2 gold crimp beads, ¹⁄₈in. (3mm) in diameter

Split ring, ¼in. (5mm) in diameter

Lobster clasp, ⅝in. (1.5cm) long

Scissors

Chain-nosed pliers

Simple matching earrings (*opposite*) have been assembled using the same beads and stones, threaded onto copper wire. A glass bead sandwiched between two turquoise chips threaded onto an end pin hangs freely beneath.

1. Cut the tiger tail into three lengths, each measuring 24in. (60cm). Thread one of the faux turquoise beads centrally onto the three strands. Add one of the larger glass beads either side.

2. Open up the three strands of tiger tail and thread each of these strands with nine turquoise chips. Bring the strands together again and thread all three through another glass bead.

3. Continue building up the necklace in the same way, adding two more oval faux turquoise beads either side of the original central one. Follow each one with three strands of turquoise chips.

4. When you have threaded five large faux turquoise beads and six sets of turquoise chips, add three smaller glass beads interspacing each one with two turquoise chips. Add the crimp bead and follow with one last glass bead. At this point you need to pull the tiger tail taut, pushing all the beads along so that no tiger tail is showing.

5. Bring the tiger tail around the split ring and back on itself through the last glass bead and the crimp that was threaded on before it. Pull the tiger tail threads one by one until they are tightly around the split ring, crimp the bead firmly with the chain-nosed pliers to secure. Cut off the excess, leaving approximately $1/4$in. (5mm) to thread through the adjacent bead. You may find it easier to thread the wire through a further bead before pulling and cutting.

6. Repeat on the other end of the necklace, threading the tiger tail through the ring on the lobster clasp before crimping the bead firmly to secure.

Variation (*below*) This striking deep blue necklace is also threaded on three strands of tiger tail. Here silver foil-lined beads have been used as accents along the iridescent seed bead thread, which is punctuated by smaller round foil-lined beads. There are endless ways of using multiple stringing, but the important things to consider are color and the use of contrasting sizes of beads.

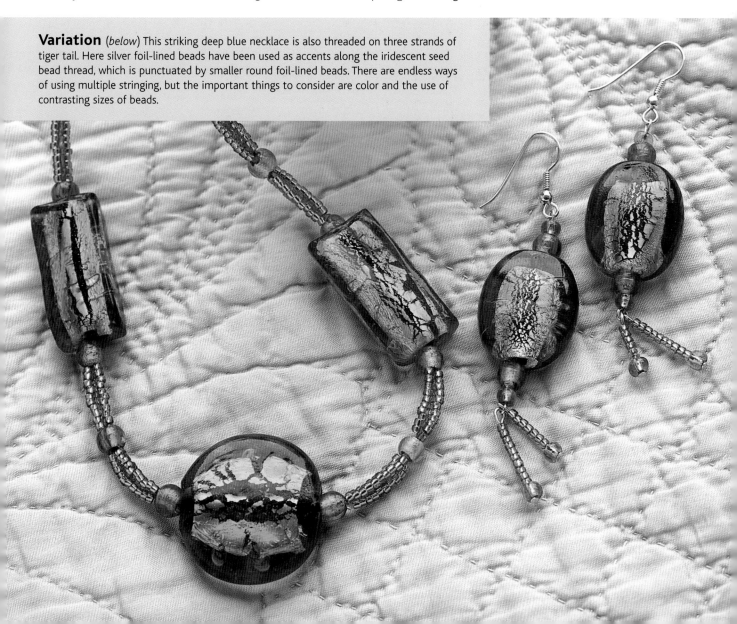

Carved lapis lazuli flower necklace

Lapis lazuli is one of the most beautiful semi-precious stones, and the incredible rich blue pigment from the powdered stone has been highly prized by artists throughout history. It has been a sought-after stone for jewelry and is mined in only two places in the world – Africa and Afghanistan. Because of its rarity, it has been traded around the world for centuries and many examples of historic pieces of jewelry using lapis can be seen in museums and galleries around the globe. The flower beads used here are carved by women in Afghanistan using traditional techniques. A little more expensive than other semi-precious stones, lapis lazuli is still affordable for a treasured piece of jewelry.

Technique:
SLIDING KNOT ON LEATHER CORD

Level of difficulty:
SIMPLE

Estimated making time:
1 HOUR

you will need

6 carved lapis flower beads (or similar), approximately 1in. (2.5cm) in diameter

9 solid silver spacer beads

3 reeded lapis beads, ³/₄in. (2cm) long

2 small spacer lapis beads

1 yard (1m) leather cord, ¹/₁₆in. (1mm) thick

Scissors

1. Thread the six flower beads onto the leather cord, interspacing them with the silver beads.

2. At each end of the flower beads add the reeded and spacer lapis beads, also with the silver spacer beads between. Tie a single knot close to the last bead and repeat on the other side.

3. Thread the last reeded bead onto the overlapping ends of the leather cord, pull until the circle of the necklace is approximately 24in. (60cm) long, including the overlapped ends.

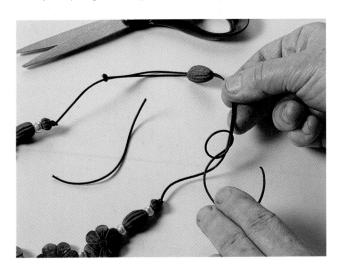

TIP Always check that the holes in your chosen beads are large enough to take the leather cord. If they are a little too tight, you can enlarge them slightly with the careful use of a small file.

4. To make the sliding knot, hold the cords parallel and turn the end around on itself in a circle. From behind, put the end through the circle and pull tightly to make the knot. Repeat on the other side and cut off the remaining leather, leaving approximately $1/8$in. (3mm) spare.

Variations (*below*) Make a simple bracelet to match the necklace using leftover beads threaded onto beading elastic. The accompanying earrings are made using silver end pins that are threaded through the beads and looped onto the fish hook findings. It is always best to use sterling silver findings to match the quality of the lapis stone.

Lemon jade and serpentine necklace

This elegant and unusually colored necklace uses small, flattened, round beads of lemon jade, which are subtly complemented by the larger, flattened, oval darker green serpentine beads. These are all threaded onto three or four strands of green-gold tiger tail. The beads are spaced apart with use of gold-colored crimp beads, thus making the colored tiger tail an important part of the design. Jade is commonly believed to bring good luck, so this may be a necklace to wear for an important occasion, such as sitting for an exam or for a stage or concert performance.

Technique:
USING CRIMP BEADS

Level of difficulty:
SIMPLE TECHNIQUE BUT SOME SKILL INVOLVED

Estimated making time:
1¼ HOURS

you will need

8 flattened round/cylindrical lemon jade beads, approximately ⅝ in. (1.5cm) in diameter/length (if you buy these on a string they will be graded according to size, so use smaller beads for the ends of the necklace)

3 large flattened oval serpentine beads, approximately 1⅜ in. (3.5cm) in length

Green-gold tiger tail, size 0.38mm (if you can't get the right color in this size, buy a larger size but use fewer strands)

2 end crimps with ring

22 gold-colored crimp tubes, ⅛ in. (3mm) in diameter

2 gold-colored jump rings, ⅜ in. (7mm) in diameter

Chain-nosed pliers

Scissors

Lemon jade earrings (*opposite*)
These pretty lemon jade and freshwater pearl earrings are made in a similar way using two strands of tiger tail. These are threaded with one small jade bead and a couple of pearls before being looped around long, green-dyed pearls and secured with crimp tubes.

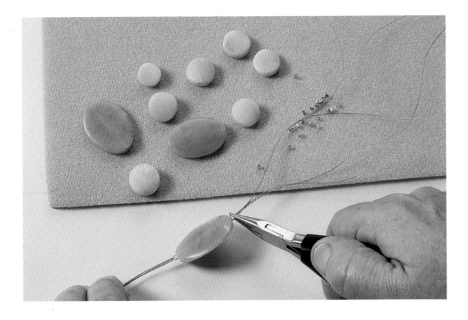

1. Cut three or four lengths of the tiger tail, depending on its thickness and the size of the holes through the beads (check that the number of strands used will all fit into the end crimp). Thread the largest serpentine bead onto the center of all the strands, followed by a crimp tube on each side. Press the crimps firmly with the pliers to hold the serpentine in place.

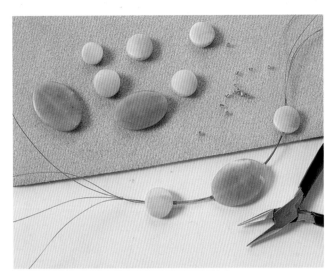

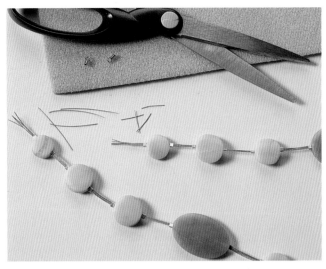

2. Thread on another crimp tube and press to secure 1in. (2.5cm) away from the previous crimp bead. Add a lemon jade bead followed by another crimp, and press with the pliers to secure.

3. Leave a ³/₄ in. (2cm) space before following on with crimp, serpentine, crimp. Leave another ³/₄ in. (2cm) gap before adding the three lemon jade beads, all spaced with the crimps. Reduce the space between them gradually as well as the size of the beads. Repeat on the other side of the central serpentine bead until all the beads are threaded symmetrically.

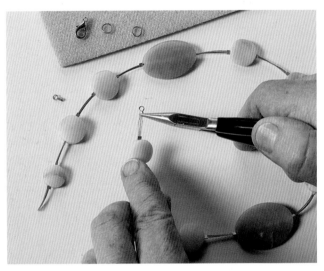

4. Cut off the tiger tail strands together approximately ¹/₂ in. (1cm) from the final crimp. Push all the tiger tail ends neatly into the crimp end and press very firmly with the pliers to secure the ends. Finally, add the jump rings to the rings on the ends of the crimps and add the lobster clasp to one side.

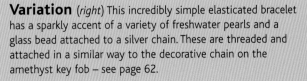

Variation (*right*) This incredibly simple elasticated bracelet has a sparkly accent of a variety of freshwater pearls and a glass bead attached to a silver chain. These are threaded and attached in a similar way to the decorative chain on the amethyst key fob – see page 62.

Variation (*below*) This amazonite and crystal bead necklace is really beautiful, and once again the skill is in choosing the right color and bead combinations. Here, silvery-pink tiger tail and silver crimp tubes have been used to space the Swarovski bicone turquoise crystals between the large lozenge-shaped amazonite carved beads.

Amethyst key fob with glass bead cluster

A simple effective project, these key fobs with the semi-precious stone pendants were bought from a crystal shop and were surprisingly inexpensive. The cluster of beads has been threaded securely onto the existing chain. Amethyst, a truly beautiful crystal, is said to have the quality of promoting peace and calm – what perfect characteristics to possess whilst driving! It's also extremely practical – due to its size, it would be much harder to lose your keys. The other fob shown is a slice of dyed agate.

Technique:
ATTACHING BEADS TO A CHAIN

Level of difficulty:
SIMPLE BUT FIDDLY

Estimated making time:
1 HOUR

you will need

Shop-bought key fob with chunky amethyst pendant or similar

10 assorted mauve toned glass beads

7 small amethyst beads

7 long end pins

Chain-nosed pliers

Round-nosed pliers

Wire cutters

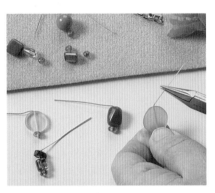

1. Thread the beads in varying combinations onto the end pins – some singles, some doubles with the small amethysts at the base.

2. Use the chain-nosed pliers to bend the end pins at a right angle, then change to the round-nosed pliers to form a tight loop. Push the end through a link of the chain and wind it around on itself tightly a couple of times, then cut off the excess. This will ensure the beads won't detach themselves with constant use. Add the rest of the beads equidistantly along the chain.

(*left*) This photo shows how the beads are attached along the length of chain.
(*right*) Here a blue agate pendant has been threaded onto a suede and blue leather necklace. Matching glass beads have been added in a similar fashion to the blue suede thong (see page 27).

Wrapped amazonite pendant with moonstones and amazonite chips

It is claimed that amazonite, a stunning blue-green stone, reduces worries and it is believed to filter electromagnetic pollution. Moonstone is thought to ease stress and calm emotion, so altogether this necklace could prove to be a rather useful item in our present day lives. The beautiful pendant-shaped amazonite stone has been wrapped with an anodized aluminum wire as a clever way of fixing it to the necklace. Small, round moonstone beads have been threaded between the amazonite chips and magically seem to have an inner glow.

Technique:
WRAPPING A STONE WITH WIRE

Level of difficulty:
REQUIRES SOME SKILL

Estimated making time:
1¹/₂ HOURS

you will need

72 amazonite chips

17 round moonstone beads 6mm

20in. (50cm) length of tiger tail, 0.38mm diameter

2 silver crimp tubes, ¹/₈in. (3mm) in diameter

1 silver jump ring, ³/₈in. (8mm)

1 lobster clasp

Pendant-shaped amazonite stone, approximately 1³/₈in. (3.5cm) long

Approximately 54in (1.5m) length of lilac-colored aluminum wire, 0.4mm in diameter

Wire cutters

Round-nosed pliers

Chain-nosed pliers

1. Thread six amazonite chips centrally on to the length of tiger tail. Add a single moonstone bead to each side.

2. Continue threading symmetrically from the center, adding six sets of five chips interspersed with a moonstone bead either side. After adding the penultimate moonstone on each end, add three chips followed by a crimp tube and a final moonstone bead. Take the tiger tail over the small ring on the lobster clasp and back through the last moonstone, the crimp, and the last chip. Pull the tiger tail firmly to tighten all the beads, then press very firmly using the chain-nosed pliers to secure. Cut off the excess tiger tail.

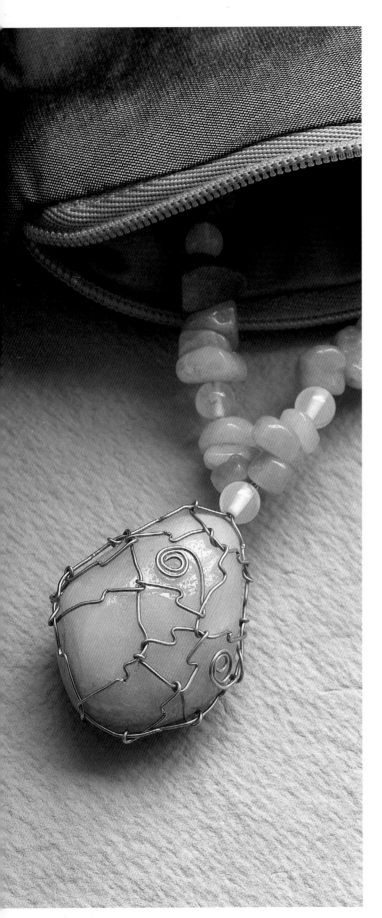

3. Fold the aluminum wire in half over the necklace halfway along the row of centrally spaced amazonite chips. Bring the two ends of wire together and thread the two strands through a moonstone bead.

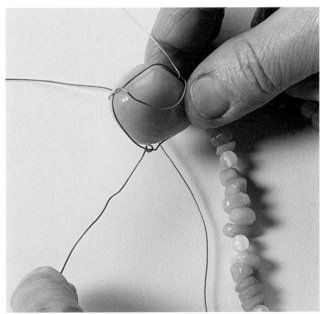

4. Place the top (the narrow part) of the amazonite stone against the moonstone bead and open out the wire. Bring it around the pendant and turn it over itself at the base, then begin to wind around the stone.

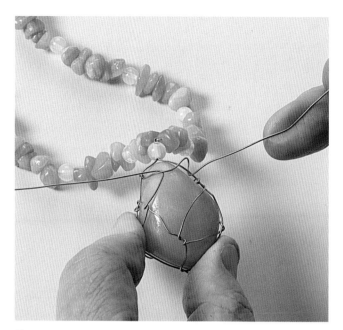

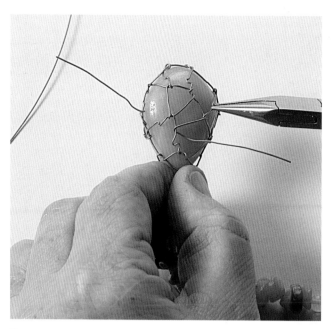

5. Continue winding the two lengths of wire around the stone forming a net to enclose the stone. As each piece crosses the other, secure it by twisting one around the other.

6. Cut off the ends of the wire, leaving about 2¹/₂in. (6cm) free. Using the chain-nosed pliers, grip sections of the wire and turn the pliers to make a decorative bend in the wire. Do this all around the pendant to tighten the wire against the stone. Turn the ends of the wire into sprirals, by winding them with the round-nosed pliers, then use the chain-nosed pliers to press the spirals flat against the stone.

Variation This variation shows a beautiful piece of rose quartz encased within fine silver wire. To enhance this further, a small lilac-colored bead has been threaded onto the wire during the wrapping process. Make sure you wrap wire close to the outer edges of the quartz, as this will enable you to attach the wire from the rest of the necklace.

CHAPTER 3

the glory of glass beads

It is impossible not to marvel at the amazing variety and artistry of glass beads. As you select them for your projects, you will realize that many are still hand-made. These skills and techniques are a continuation of a historic tradition, especially in Europe. Glass beads have always been traded around the world, so you will find tribes in Africa wearing beads that have originally been made in Bohemia. Some bead shops offer inexpensive packs of a bead mix. This is a good way to start, so buy a few packs and spend a little time sorting through and working out interesting bead combinations. Small seed beads, which are available in a huge variety of colors, are very useful, particularly to thread between decorated feature beads. Recycling old necklaces is a good way to build up your glass bead collection.

Right: Glass beads have been made and traded through the ages and form an interesting part of our cultural history. Some decorated examples are exquisite in their technique and design, and so many are now readily available from good bead suppliers.

Millefiori pendant

Millefiori literally means "a thousand flowers" and when you look carefully at millefiori beads you can see what an accurate description that is. It is an intricate, specialized technique originating in Italy whereby colored glass is fused together in the form of many beautiful flowers. You may have seen pretty glass paperweights using this magical technique. Here, a striking millefiori pendant is complemented by a matching millefiori chip strand necklace. As the glass beads are so busy and colorful, this jewelry would look best worn with a simple, single-colored outfit.

Technique:
ATTACHING A PENDANT

Level of difficulty:
SIMPLE

Estimated making time:
LESS THAN 1 HOUR

you will need

1 gold-colored eye pin

Millefiori glass disc pendant, approximately 1^1/$_2$in. (4cm) in diameter

24in. (60cm) tiger tail

Approximately 88 millefiori chips

2 small, round millefiori beads for the ends

2 clamshell calottes

2 small gold-colored crimp beads, ^{1}/$_{16}$in. (1.5mm) in diameter

Split ring

Snake clasp

Chain-nosed pliers

Round-nosed pliers

Scissors

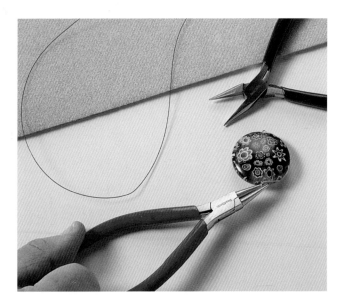

1. Push the eye pin through the hole in the pendant. Using the chain-nosed pliers, bend over the protruding end at a right angle. Change to the round-nosed pliers and bend into a small closed loop.

2. Thread the pendant centrally onto the tiger tail, then add approximately 44 millefiori chips on either side, finishing with a round millefiori bead.

3. Push the tiger tail through the clamshell calottes and then through the crimp beads. Use the chain-nosed pliers to push the bead up against the calotte and press to flatten. Cut off the excess tiger tail and close the calottes.

4. Attach the split ring to one calotte and the snake clasp to the other by closing the ring on the calottes.

Variation (*above and right*) This pretty millefiori necklace is made in the same way as the main project, but many smaller charms are added along its length. The millefiori chips and tiny round beads can be bought fairly inexpensively on long threads. The matching earrings have been made using more similarly toned beads. The heart and other beads have been threaded onto eye pins so they can swing freely from the base.

Recycled glass beads on patinated copper chain

There is something so beautiful about this simple necklace – the clear sea green of the glass beads against the patinated copper makes a perfect color combination. Such recycled beads often come from Africa and are part of the global bead trade; they may have originated in Europe and are often quite old. You just need to perfect the technique of threading the beads with wire and looping each end over a link in the chain to join up all the beads. Copper wire is soft and easy to work, and the same principle applies to the chain, which is not difficult to cut.

Technique:
THREADING ON CHAIN

Level of difficulty:
SIMPLE

Estimated making time:
1 HOUR

you will need

1 yard (1m) copper chain (with small and large links if possible)

Soft copper wire, 1/32 in. (0.5mm) thick

6 lozenge-shaped green glass beads with large holes

6 square faceted beads, either sand blasted or with a matte finish, with large holes

Wire cutters
Chain-nosed pliers
Round-nosed pliers

Matching bracelet (*opposite*) This is made in the same way as the necklace, using the smaller beads interspersed with copper charms and one large feature bead. A copper toggle clasp has been used to open and close the bracelet. This is easily attached using copper jump rings.

1. Using the wire cutters, cut the chain into four-link lengths. If using a chain with smaller links, leave one at either end of the large links.

2. Cut a length of copper wire to fit through the large glass beads, leaving ¹/₂ in. (1cm) standing proud on each side. Bend the wire at right angles using the chain-nosed pliers. Change to the round-nosed pliers and turn the wire into a loop. Cut off any excess wire and turn around the small chain link back into the glass bead for security.

3. At the other end of the wire, form a similar loop and bend around a new piece of the chain in the same way. Add a smaller bead to the other end of this second length of chain. Continue in this manner, attaching the two sizes of bead alternately onto the chain, until you have one of each type of bead remaining.

4. Thread a length of wire into the last large bead and form a loop as before, but this time attach it to the two small links at each end of the assembled chain. Thread a wire through the small remaining bead and attach to the loop at the base of the larger pendant bead. Bend the excess wire at the base of this bead into a small tight loop to finish.

Variation (*above*) A smaller chain has been used for this version of the necklace. An eclectic collection of smokey-pink glass beads has been threaded with wire to form part of the chain or threaded with an end pin to suspend the bead from the chain. An interesting feature of this necklace is the way that a second chain has been attached with matching jump rings to make an elegant double necklace at the lower part. A small pendant of three wire-linked beads finishes the necklace at the center of the lower chain.

Multicolored glass necklace

This jolly necklace is great fun to make. The beads came in a pack labeled "assorted Indian beads." Buying beads in a pack is a good idea as they are often inexpensive, and are themed either by color, origin of the beads, or shape. You will often have enough beads in a single pack to make a number of pieces of jewelry, and if you buy two or more packs you can mix and match. For this necklace, make sure the beads have holes that are sufficiently large to allow fairly thick cord to be threaded through. Two complementary cords are used to thread alternately through the beads, and tying a knot between each bead allows them to move freely along the cord between knots. Two necklaces are shown here – the instructions explain how to make the green version.

Technique:
KNOTTING TWO CORDS

Level of difficulty:
SIMPLE

Estimated making time:
LESS THAN 1 HOUR

you will need

1 yard (1m) olive green satin cord (also known as rat tail), $^1/_{16}$ in. (1mm) thick

1 yard (1m) lime green woven cord, $^1/_{16}$ in. (1mm) thick

16 Indian glass beads in assorted sizes (or more if you want a longer necklace)

2 coils and loops, $^1/_3$ x $^1/_8$ in. (7 x 3mm), for enclosing the cord

Clasp

Split ring

Small jump ring

Chain-nosed pliers

Round-nosed pliers

Scissors

> **TIP** When using chunky beads, check the edges of bead holes are smooth, particularly when dealing with metal ethnic beads. If the edges are sharp, they may cut through cord. File these edges down using the fine-grade or wet or dry sandpaper.

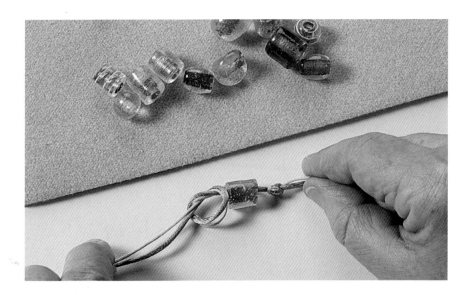

1. Lay the two lengths of cord side by side and knot the cords together 1$^1/_4$ in. (3cm) from one end. Thread the first bead onto the rat tail and allow the bead some movement on the cord before tying the second knot.

2. Thread the next bead onto the lime green cord and tie a similar knot. Continue in this manner, threading the beads onto alternate cords between knots.

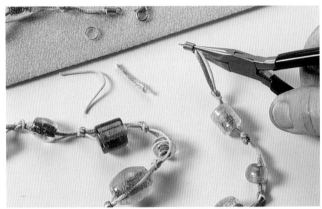

3. Continue threading the beads until all are used up, then cut the cords so that each has a 1¹/₄in. (3cm) length left at the end (the same as at the beginning of each cord). Push the two ends of the cord into the coil and loop. Using the chain-nosed pliers with ends pointing into the coil, grip the end coil and press it against the cord to secure.

(*above*) This detail shows how the beads and knots are spaced apart, allowing movement within the necklace.

4. Attach the split ring onto the ring at the end of the coil; attach the other smaller ring to the coil at the other end. Attach the clasp to this smaller ring to finish the necklace.

Variation (*above*) This lovely necklace has no clasp as the beads are threaded onto a leather cord long enough to reach over your head. A delicate shot rayon ribbon in a complementary color has been threaded through some of the beads, allowing it to weave gently along the necklace. The ribbon and leather cord are simply tied together in a small, neat knot to secure.

Cluster of blue glass beads on knotted suede thong

Technique:
ATTACHING BEADS WITH END PINS

Level of difficulty:
FIDDLY

Estimated making time:
1¹/₂ HOURS

This unusual blue suede thong can be adapted to wear in a number of ways. Wear it as a necklace loosely tied in front (the weight of the beads will keep it in place) or more adventurously as a stunning tie around the waist of light linen trousers or a pretty summery dress. This technique can lend itself to many variations, for example double up the suede with a contrasting leather or velvet ribbon. Attaching the beads onto rings enclosed in the single knots means they are quite secure.

you will need

Blue suede thong, ¹/₈in. (3mm) wide and 48in. (1.2m) long

9 copper jump rings, ¹/₄in. (5mm) in diameter

2 copper end calottes

Eclectic selection of 30 blue glass beads and a few matching buttons

15 copper end pins

5 eye pins

Round-nosed pliers

Chain-nosed pliers

Wire cutters

TIP You can often buy packs of assorted glass beads from suppliers – just add a few tiny buttons and some dyed mother-of-pearl chips to the cluster for extra interest.

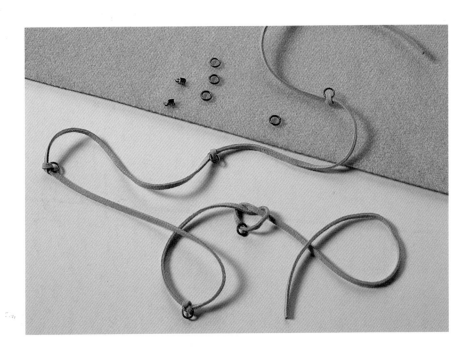

1. Tie seven equidistant knots into the suede thong, incorporating a jump ring into each knot.

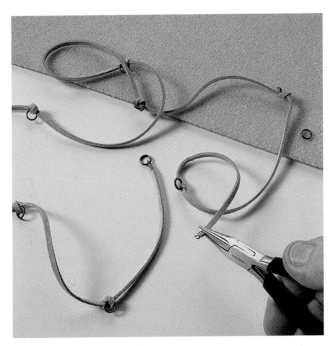

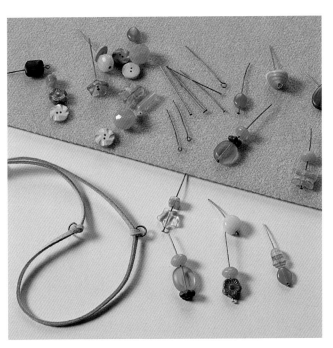

2. Enclose both ends of the suede into the copper calottes, press firmly with the chain-nosed pliers, and attach jump rings onto the calotte ends.

3. Thread a selection of the beads onto the end pins, using some single beads and some double. Thread some of the beads onto eye pins so that you can add a further bead onto the loop below to swing freely.

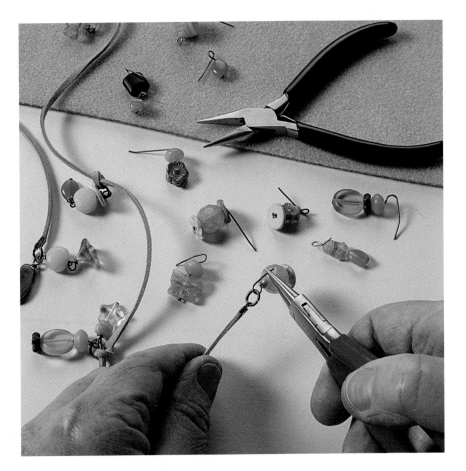

4. Bend over the end of the remaining end-pin wire at a right angle with the chain-nosed pliers, then use the round-nosed pliers to make a small loop. Before closing it, thread through the jump ring in the knot, and press to close securely. Attach these threaded beads onto the knot jump ring in pairs and singly all along the length of the suede and onto the rings at both ends.

Variation This pretty two-tone suede necklace is also simple to make, with the cluster of assorted pink and red beads attached to three lengths of copper chain. In turn, these are attached to the suede using copper jump rings. This is a good design for using up a collection of beads left over from other projects.

Foil-lined glass heart pendant on ribbon

This charming heart-shaped pendant is a perfect project for a young girl to make. Threading with ribbon is an easy, effective, and stylish alternative to using cord or chain. The ribbon is held in a folding clasp which has tiny teeth to grip the fabric firmly. If you take care to fold the ribbon carefully together so it is the right width for the clasp, it will make a secure and neat ending. Two kinds of ribbon have been used together here – a narrow pink organdie offset against the beautiful tones of a silk dip-dyed version. These have been thoughtfully chosen to complement the subtle color and shimmering quality of the foil-lined glass beads. When choosing ribbons and beads to match, always make sure you have one with you when you choose the other.

Technique:
WORKING WITH RIBBON

Level of difficulty:
SIMPLE

Estimated making time:
LESS THAN 1 HOUR

you will need

3 fire-polished faceted glass beads, 1/4 in. (5mm) long

2 small square mauve foil-lined glass beads, 1/4 in. (5mm) long]

1 green foil-lined glass heart, 3/4 in. (2cm) long

1 mauve foil-lined glass diamond, 2/3 in. (15mm) long

Pink organdie ribbon, 24in. (60cm) long, 1/4 in. (5mm) wide

Dip-dyed silk ribbon, 24in. (60cm) long, 1/2 in. (1cm) wide

2 short end pins, 1 1/2 in. (4cm) long

1 long eye pin, 3in. (7.5cm) long

1 silver closed jump ring

3 jump rings, two 1/4 in. (5mm) and one 1/3 in. (7mm) in diameter

2 1/2 in. (6cm) length of silver chain

2 ribbon clasps

1 bolt ring, 1/3 in. (8mm) in diameter

Scissors

Chain-nosed pliers

Round-nosed pliers

1. Thread the small faceted glass beads onto the two shorter end pins, followed by the square foil-lined beads. Use the chain-nosed pliers to turn the protruding wire at a right angle. Thread the heart, followed by the remaining crystal and the diamond, onto the long eye pin and bend the wire over at a right angle in the same way.

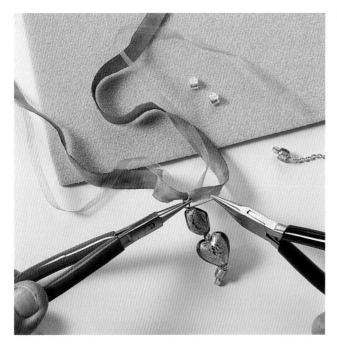

2. Thread the closed jump ring centrally onto the two lengths of ribbon. Use the round-nosed pliers to bend the longer eye pin over and through the jump ring in a small loop. Hold the loop with the round-nosed pliers whilst turning the remaining wire around on itself with the chain-nosed pliers to secure. Attach one of the smaller end pins and beads to the ring below the heart in the same manner. Attach the remaining end pin to the end of the silver chain.

3. Make sure that the ribbon ends are cut neatly and fold them over so that they are the same width as the clasp. Push them in and press the clasp gently with the chain-nosed pliers, adjusting them for a perfect fit. Press firmly to secure.

TIP To attach a jump ring, hold the two sides of the metal and gently push one away from the other in a sideways movement, attach it, and then pull back the end to meet the other, bringing it slightly further forward before pushing back to the final position. Never pull the two ends away from each other as this weakens the metal.

4. Attach one larger and one smaller jump ring to each of the rings on the ribbon clasps. Use the second small ring to attach the silver chain. Attach the bolt ring to the smaller jump ring.

Variation (*below*) These pretty matching earrings are very simple to make, with a slightly different combination of beads threaded in the same way onto eye pins and end pins. They are simply looped over fish hook earring findings. Wear them with the pendant for a formal occasion.

Chinese enamel flower
swing necklace

This is a lovely simple project that can be made to any length you like. There is no clasp so you must make it long enough to fit over your head, but if you make it twice as long you could wear it doubled up. The little Chinese enamel flowers, although different in style to the foil-lined glass beads, work so well with them. If you browse in a bead store, you will find an incredible variety of beads that you could assemble in a similar way. This necklace is so quick to make – try making a few and wearing them all together.

Technique:
THREADING WITH SEED BEADS

Level of difficulty:
VERY SIMPLE

Estimated making time:
LESS THAN 1 HOUR

you will need

Large quantity of lime-green seed beads, approximately 1/8 in. (3mm) in diameter

10 rectangular matte foil-lined green glass beads, 1in. (2.5cm) long

5 Chinese enamel flower beads, 3/4 in. (2cm) in diameter

5 gold-colored end pins

1 yard (1m) green tiger tail

2 gold-colored crimp beads

Chain-nosed pliers

Round-nosed pliers

Scissors

TIP Working with tiger tail is really easy as it is firm and will easily thread through small holes, acting like a fine needle.

1. Push the end pins through the enamel beads, then use the chain-nosed pliers to bend the extending wire at a right angle. Change to the round-nosed pliers and make a small tight loop, cut off the excess, and push the cut end back a small way into the hole in the bead.

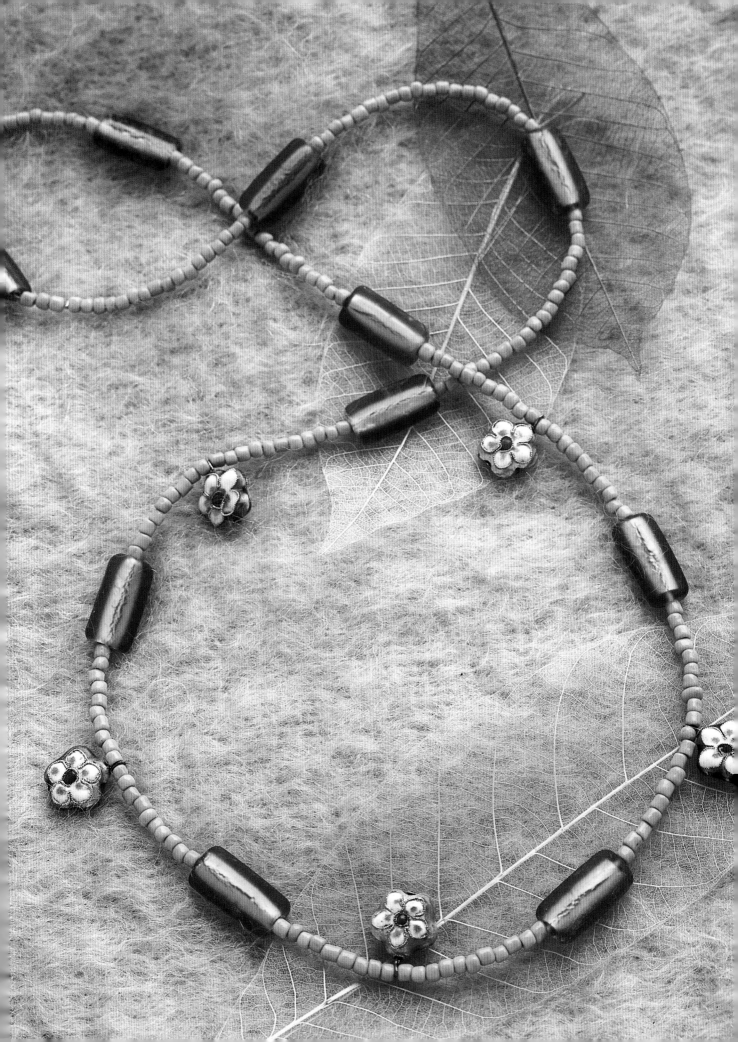

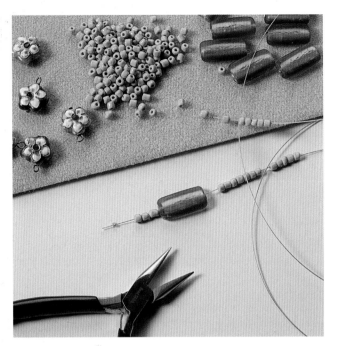

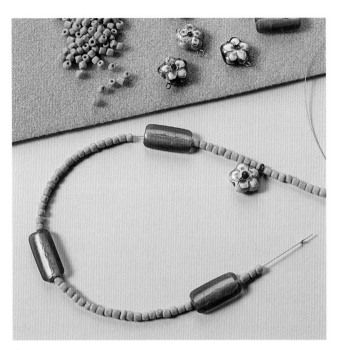

2. Press a crimp bead on to the end of the tiger tail to prevent the beads falling off. Start by threading on three seed beads, add a rectangular glass bead followed another 20 seed beads, then add another rectangular glass bead.

3. Add 20 more seed beads followed by a glass bead. Next, add 10 seed beads and thread on an enamel flower. Add 10 more seed beads before threading the next glass bead.

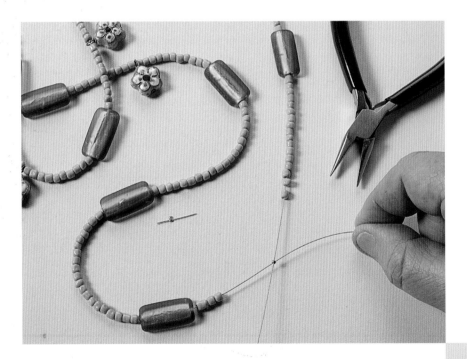

4. Continue in this manner, inserting the four remaining enamel flowers midway between the glass beads. Add the remaining two glass beads interspersed with seed beads, then finish by adding 18 more seed beads. Move the beads along away from the crimp, cut this off and thread the two ends through the second crimp bead from opposite sides. Pull the tiger tail so that there is no space between the beads. Press tightly with the chain-nosed pliers to secure, then cut off the excess tiger tail leaving about ¹/₂in. (1cm) on each side. Thread this through the adjacent beads to hide.

Variation (*right*) The unusually colored luster beads look really rich and stylish threaded with shimmering gold seed beads and gold foil-lined glass teardrop beads. You may like to make a wilder necklace by using an eclectic mix of beads on a single-color seed bead thread.

Stranded seed bead necklace with millefiori bead accents

Technique:
JOINING MULTI STRANDS

Level of difficulty:
SIMPLE, BUT REQUIRES PATIENCE

Estimated making time:
2¹/₂ HOURS

Although the individual elements in this unusual necklace are small, using, in effect, five necklaces joined together makes a bold statement. The small pink seed beads are taken from an old vintage necklace, and they have a pleasing irregularity of shape and color which adds to the design. The plain glass and millefiori beads threaded into three of the strands are carefully spaced so that they don't correspond on each separate strand, thus creating a random effect.

you will need

Large handful of medium pink seed beads

Approximately 44 tiny pink seed beads

6 pink glass cylindrical beads, ³/₄in. (2cm) long

4 white flower-decorated glass lamp beads, ⁵/₈in. (12mm)

6 pink heart-shaped millefiori beads, ¹/₂in. (1cm) long

120in. (3m) length of tiger tail

2 copper clamshell calottes

1 copper jump rings, ³/₈in. (7mm) in diameter

1 copper jump ring, ¹/₄in. (5mm) in diameter

1 lobster clasp

10 large crimp tubes, for securing ends of tiger tail

2 copper crimp beads, ¹/₈in. (3mm) in diameter

Chain-nosed pliers

Round-nosed pliers

Scissors

TIP To make a multi-stranded necklace sit well, all the strands need to be threaded with a varying number of beads so that they are all slightly differing lengths. This ensures that when they are all threaded, they lie separated and thus display the beads to their best advantage.

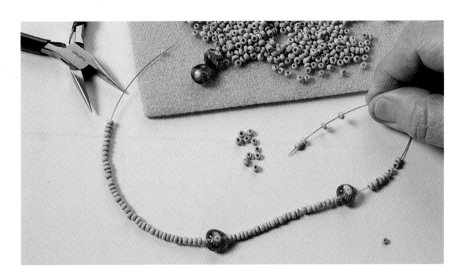

1. Cut the tiger tail into five 24in. (60cm) lengths. Use the chain-nosed pliers to attach a crimp bead at one end of each length (this is to stop the beads falling off as you thread them). Using one tiger tail strand, thread on 40 pink seed beads followed by millefiori heart. Add approximately 26 seed beads and follow with another heart. Thread all the hearts in this manner. When the last one is in place, add 40 seed beads to complete the strand. Add a crimp tube to hold the beads in place while you thread the next strand.

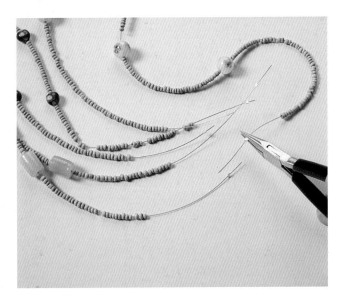

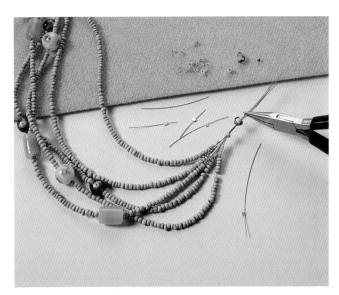

2. Thread up the second strand with the cylindrical glass beads. Start with approximately 30 seed beads and intersperse the larger beads, finishing with 30 seed beads at the end. Thread the third strand with the white lamp beads with 60 seed beads at either end and approximately 40 between them. Always remember to add the crimp tube for security – this should be at least 4in. (10cm) away from the first and last bead.

3. Thread up the fourth and fifth strands of tiger tail purely with seed beads. Thread 250 beads onto one strand and 220 onto the other. As before, press the securing crimp tubes well away from the last threaded beads. Now that all the strands are threaded, you need to cut off the crimps very carefully. Be sure not to let any beads fall off. Thread a few tiny pink seed beads onto the end of each strand. Next, thread all the ends through a larger pink seed bead, then push all the strands of tiger tail through the hole in the middle of the calotte and through the copper crimp bead. Use the chain-nosed pliers to pull all the strands tightly through the calotte and the crimp. Press the crimp with pliers to secure and cut off the excess tiger tail.

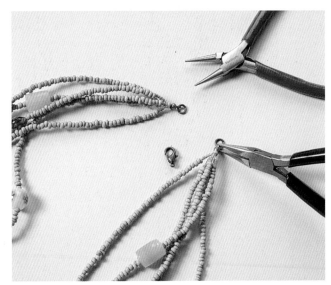

Variation (*above*) These stylish bracelets using old seed beads are simply threaded onto beading elastic secured with a crimp. For added interest, small metal spacer beads are threaded either side of the feature beads. Making bracelets is a good way of using up beads left over from other projects.

4. Use the round-nosed pliers to bring the loop of the calotte around the larger and smaller jump ring at each end of the necklace, then close using the chain-nosed pliers. Open the smaller jump ring and close around the small ring attachment on the lobster clasp.

Variation (*below*) A three-strand necklace of white seed beads which have been interspersed with faceted plastic beads recycled from a 1930s necklace. Plastic beads have the added advantage of being indestructable. The matching earrings have been made by threading the seed beads and the pink plastic beads onto a wire ring. The two beads at the base have been suspended using end pins and eye pins.

Furnace glass beads on chiffon ribbon

An ideal project for beginners, threading beads onto a knotted ribbon is a simple and stylish way of holding the beads in place. There's no need for any metal clasps – just tie a bow to wear the necklace and untie it to take it off! Knotting is a traditional way of threading pearls onto a fine silk thread, as it prevents them from rubbing against each other and thus guards against damage. The glass beads used here have holes large enough to thread chiffon ribbon through. Any bead will work, but it is always worth checking the size of the hole first. Use a thinner ribbon for smaller beads. With the number of glass beads available and the endless variety of ribbon, the possibilities are endless.

Technique:
KNOTTING RIBBON

Level of difficulty:
VERY SIMPLE

Estimated making time:
LESS THAN 1 HOUR

You will need

Chenille needle
2 yards (2m) green chiffon ribbon
Assorted glass beads with large holes in shades of blue, green, turquoise, and wine
Scissors

Tip Sometimes the inside of a glass bead can be rough and may damage the ribbon. Check by threading a small length of ribbon through to see if it catches. You can try filing it smooth with a small round file, but this is laborious so it is best to choose more suitable beads.

1. Thread the end of the ribbon through the chenille needle, thread through the large green bead, and position it into the center of the ribbon. Tie a knot on each side of this bead.

2. Working on each side of the central bead, thread another bead, and knot the ribbon as before. Continue adding more beads in this way until your necklace is the required length. You will need to make sure there is approximately 8in. (20cm) of ribbon left at each end in order to tie into a bow.

Variation (*above*) These unusual small striped beads are also made of glass and look like layers of colored sand. Try to choose a ribbon that subtly enhances the color and pattern of the beads used.

Variation (*above*) These natural toned and carved wooden beads have been threaded onto a dark brown satin ribbon. Wood is a lighter material to wear and it won't drag the ribbon.

Chunky amber and pewter necklace

A statement necklace is an essential in every woman's wardrobe – and for the impact it makes, this big-bead showpiece is surprisingly inexpensive and easy to create. Offering a strong but elegant presence right through from day to evening, the necklace uses very simple glass, plastic, and metal beads in classic terra-cotta, amber, and silver, with an oversized clasp that adds scale too. This project shows how to use a beading board, which provides an easy way for you to decide the order of the beads before threading them.

Technique:
THREADING AND CLASP FIXING

Level of difficulty:
SIMPLE

Estimated making time:
1 HOUR

you will need

Soft-cover beading board

Six types of big bead with 1/6in. (2mm) diameter holes: pewter-look oval beads, pewter-look round beads, wooden slice beads, large and small amber-look beads, and steel separator beads

1 large 11/2in. (4cm) amber bead with 1/6in. (2mm) diameter hole

Reel of 0.8 gauge miniature cable wire

Bolt ring and clasp, no smaller than 1/4in. (5 mm) in diameter

2 crimp beads

1/2in. (1 cm) French/gimp wire

Flat-nosed pliers or crimping pliers

Wire cutters

TIP When using chunky beads, check the edges of bead holes are smooth, particularly when dealing with metal ethnic beads. If the edges are sharp, they may cut through cord and the necklace with break. Smooth rough edges by filing with fine-grade or wet or dry sandpaper.

1. Cut a 25in. (75cm) length of wire. Make a "draft" of your necklace by trying out different arrangements of the beads on the beading board. Put the large amber bead in the center of the arrangement. This necklace is 16in. (40cm) long, so fill this groove on the board. Arranging is time consuming, but this stage allows you to develop the design before you commit to a final threaded version.

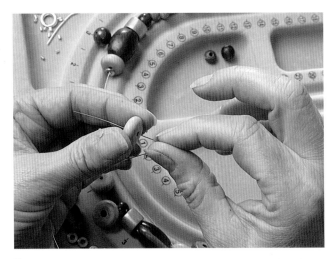

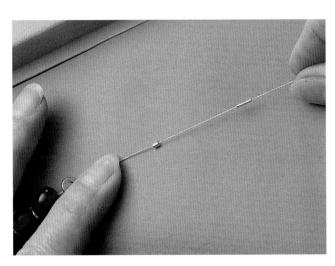

2. Using your fingers, slide the beads through the thread. Making sure the beads are centered, leave 7in. (12cm) on each side of the necklace and cut off the rest of the wire.

3. To fix the clasp, slide on a crimp bead to one end of the necklace, followed by the French wire. Take care while threading cable through the French wire – do not let it unravel.

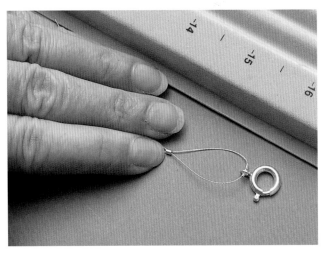

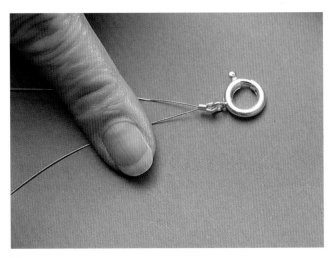

4. Now thread this wire through the soldered ring of the bolt ring and back through the crimp.

5. Pull the thread to make the crimp fit snugly. Leave about 4in. (10cm) of thread at the end.

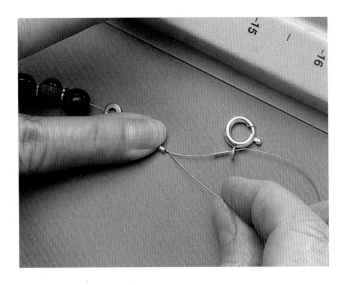

6. Feed the remainder of the thread back through as many beads as you can, to add strength to your finished necklace. Now hold down this end as a fixed point against which you pull everything taut. It's important to remember that you need a little bit of slack in a necklace so that it drapes properly and the beads aren't pushed on top of each other. If you knot between all the beads, however, this isn't necessary. Repeat steps 3–6 on the other end of the necklace, tightening the thread, avoiding gaps between the crimp bead and the last beads of the necklace.

Right: The amber glass beads give off a warm glow and their delicate translucency contrasts well with the solid silver beads.

Variation Make a pair of chunky bracelets using beads in the same colorways to create a matching set. Thread the beads on beading elastic and, if you wish, add a bow tied from narrow velvet ribbon as a decorative finishing touch.

pearls, silver, and sparkle

Every woman wants a beautiful necklace to wear on a special evening occasion, something that sparkles and glows. Freshwater and cultured pearls are available in an amazing variety of shapes, sizes, and colors. They are sold threaded onto long strings and come mainly from the Far East, particularly China and the Philippines. One string will be probably provide sufficient pearls for a few projects, especially if mixed with other elements. Shell fragments and shaped dyed pearly discs are very versatile and seem to float when threaded onto an almost invisible thread. Silver, a pure metal, is the natural companion to pearl. It can be used as charms, spacer beads, pendants, and in chain form. It is sold by weight, and look out for older chains which have the desirable patina of age.

Right: Freshwater and cultured pearls can be bought in strings of different shapes and sizes. They are often dyed subtle colors and have a wonderful, feminine quality. Make sure you buy your pearls from a sustainable source. The disks and leaf shapes shown here have been carved from large shells.

Freshwater pearl and silver chain with organdie ribbon trim

Definitely a necklace to wear for a special evening occasion, this is quite a show-stopper. The combination of silver beads and subtly toned freshwater pearls is a classic one, but this design is a little more adventurous. The organdie ribbon flowing along the sterling silver chain and the variety of shaped pearls and mother-of-pearl leaves cascading from the strand of threaded pearls make the design unique. Creating this necklace will take some time and patience, but all the techniques have been used before with other projects in the book, so don't be daunted.

Technique:
JOINING CHAIN TO TIGER TAIL

Level of difficulty:
SOME SKILL AND MUCH PATIENCE REQUIRED

Estimated making time:
3 HOURS

you will need

2 x 4^1/2in. (11cm) length of silver chain, approximately ^{1}/8in. (3mm) wide

1 large silver snake clasp

1 large silver split ring, ^{3}/8in. (8mm) in diameter

4 ribbon clamps

10^1/2in. (26cm) length of pink organdie ribbon, ^{3}/8in. (8mm) wide

16in. (40cm) length of tiger tail

7 silver jump rings, ^{1}/4in. (5mm) in diameter

2 small silver jump rings, ^{1}/8in. (3mm) in diameter

8 long silver eye pins, 2in. (5cm) in length

5 shorter silver end pins, 1^1/2in. (4cm) in length

Assorted small pearls – 30 pink and 20 natural color

22 large natural pearls, ^{3}/8in. (8mm) in diameter

6 elongated long drilled pink pearls

2 small silver crimp tubes

2 small silver beads

Round-nosed pliers

Chain-nosed pliers

Wire cutters and scissors

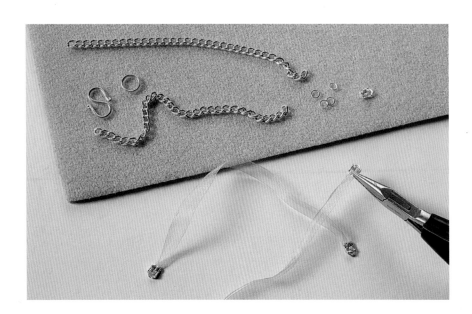

1. Cut the ribbon in half and slide each end of the two lengths into the open ribbon clamps. Using the chain-nosed pliers, press the clamp closed to hold the ribbon securely. If the ribbon is slightly wider than the clamp, you may have to fold the ribbon in half to fit (this can be slightly fiddly).

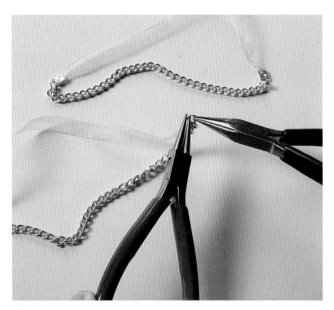

2. Open the ¹⁄₄in. (5mm) jump rings to attach to the small ring on the clamps and to the end links on each end of the two pieces of chain. Close the rings to secure. Add the large split ring to one end of the chain and the snake clasp to the other end of the chain.

3. Thread the rigid end of the tiger tail through the small hole in each pearl, starting with a small natural pearl, followed by a small pink pearl. Add a large natural pearl and continue with a small pink, two small whites, followed again by a large natural pearl. Continue in this manner until nine large pearls are threaded. Finish to match the other end with one small pink followed by a small natural pearl.

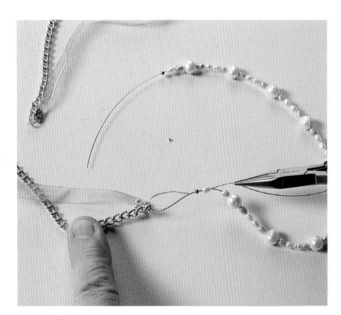

4. At each end, thread on the small silver bead followed by the tiny crimp bead. Thread the tiger tail through the last link in the chain, back through the crimp bead, through the silver bead, and through the small white pearl. Hold the chain and pull the tiger tail tight with the chain-nosed pliers. Press the crimp bead to secure. Repeat on the other end of the pearl thread.

5. Thread a variety of the pearls and silver beads onto eye pins to create eight short lengths, making each one slightly different. Bend over the end of the eye pin, cut off the excess, and turn into the beginning of a loop with the round-nosed pliers.

6. Thread the remaining pearls and silver beads onto the five small end pins. Create a loop in the same manner as before and attach to the rings on the end of the eye pins. Open up a jump ring and thread through the hole in the shell leaves. Attach these to the loops on the remaining eye pins. If you thread two leaves together, you will need to use an extra-small jump ring in order to attach more easily.

7. Attach the loop on each threaded eye pin between the two small natural pearls on the string. Bend the loop over and close firmly with the round-nosed pliers.

Variation You will also be rewarded for your patience if you decide to make a similar bracelet. Much like a classic charm bracelet, the strings of silver beads, pearls, and mother-of-pearl leaves are attached to the chain using end pins and eye pins, while the leaves are attached by using silver jump rings. When using good-quality materials, always use real silver clasps and chain for the perfect finishing touch.

Silver and freshwater pearl drop earrings

In these delicate earrings, the pink and natural tones of the freshwater pearls resemble a chain of underwater bubbles rising to the surface through the Indian pressed silver fish. Although silver is sold by weight, these fish would be relatively inexpensive as would the pearls. It is best to use real silver findings, in the form of earring hooks, end pins, and eye pins. Once you have made one pair of earrings, try other similar combinations of silver charms and beads.

Technique:
USING END PINS AND EYE PINS FOR ATTACHING TO A CHAIN

Level of difficulty:
SIMPLE BUT FIDDLY

Estimated making time:
LESS THAN 1 HOUR

you will need

2¹/₂in. (6cm) length of small linked silver chain

2 silver eye pins, 3in. (7.5cm) long

6 small silver end pins, 1¹/₂in. (4cm) long

6 large freshwater pearls, approximately ⁵/₈in. (8mm) in diameter

6 smaller pink freshwater pearls in varying sizes

2 pressed silver charm fish, approximately 1in. (2.5cm) long

Pair of solid silver earring fish hooks

Chain-nosed pliers

Round-nosed pliers

Wire cutters

Tip You will often find inexpensive old costume jewelry or odd beads in flea markets and charity shops. Make a collection that you can later recycle into a unique pair of earrings.

1. Cut the chain into two 1¹/₄in. (3cm) lengths. Put one length aside, to make the second earring. Attach one chain to the loop on the end of one large eye pin by opening and closing that loop around the first link of the chain.

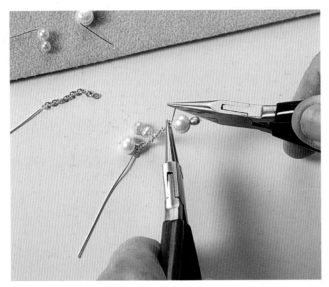

2. Thread three small end pins – the first with a single large pearl, the second with two smaller pinkish pearls, and the final one with a small pink pearl and a larger pearl. Use the chain-nosed pliers to bend the protruding wire at right angles, then change to the round-nosed pliers to form a loop, leave enough to thread through the chain and wind back on itself to secure. Using this technique, attach the single pearl to the second link of the chain, the two small pink pearls to the ninth link, and the larger and smaller pearls to the last link.

3. Thread the long eye pin with the chain attached through the silver fish charm followed by a large single pearl, to sit at the mouth of the fish.

Variation These pretty earrings are made in exactly the same way as the main project. The silver charms are left over from the silver snail pendant project featured on page 114 and the combination of pink beads is enhanced by the addition of rose quartz chips.

4. As before, bend the protruding wire at right angles and then into a loop to attach to the earring hook loop. Holding the loop with one pair of pliers, use the other pliers to twist the wire around on itself to secure; cut off the excess. Repeat the steps to make a matching earring.

Variation Using the same technique as demonstrated in the steps, why not try making these glamorous diamanté and cut-glass drop earrings? Instead of using silver charms, use diamanté roundels. Here, the smaller ones on the chain were purchased from a bead supplier, but the larger roundels have been recycled from an old necklace. The faceted glass beads at the base of the chain come from an old chandelier.

Silver snail pendant on dip-dyed satin cord

This elegant and striking pendant made from Indian silver is so effective but relatively quick and easy to make. It has been threaded onto a subtly colored dip-dyed satin cord. This cord is also known by the delightful name of rat tail! To show off the variations in color, the cord has been doubled and small silver shells are suspended from the evenly spaced knots. When using silver, in order to maintain the quality of your necklace, always try to use silver findings to match, for example the jump rings, end pins, and clasp.

Technique:
USING RAT TAIL AND CLOSED RINGS

Level of difficulty:
SIMPLE

Estimated making time:
1¹/₄ HOURS

you will need

- 2 yards (2m) dip-dyed satin cord (also known as rat tail)
- 1 large silver snail pendant or similar
- 6 smaller snail charms
- 6 short silver end pins

- 1 long silver end pin
- 7 silver closed jump rings
- 1 small silver bead
- 2 large silver calottes for ending the cord
- 2 silver split rings, one ¹/₄in. (5mm) and one ¹/₂in. (1cm) in diameter

- 1 silver snake clasp, ³/₄in. (2cm)
- Chain-nosed pliers
- Round-nosed pliers
- Wire cutters
- Scissors

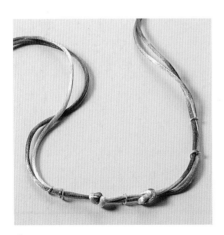

1. Cut the cord into two even lengths and lay the two pieces parallel. Thread the seven jumps rings onto the cord. Slide the fourth ring into the center and tie a knot either side so that the ring sits in a 2in. (5cm) wide space between the knots.

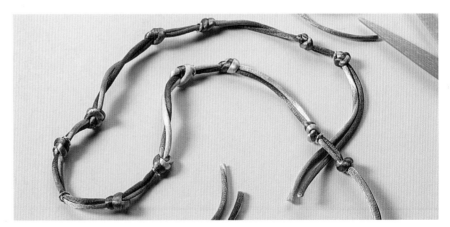

2. Working on either side of the center, place a ring after these knots, leave a ³/₄in. (2cm) gap enclosing this ring, and tie another knot. Add two more rings either side in this manner. You should have three rings on each side between two knots, but leave a larger space of 2in. (5cm) between the last two knots. Cut off the extra cord on either side 4in. (10cm) from the final knots.

This shows how the silver rings and smaller shells are attached to the double cord.

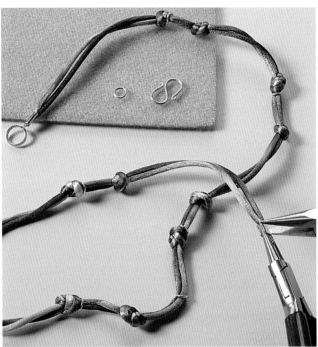

3. Enclose and secure the double end of the cord with the calottes, then add the small split ring on one side and the larger onto the other. Thread the snake clasp through the smaller ring.

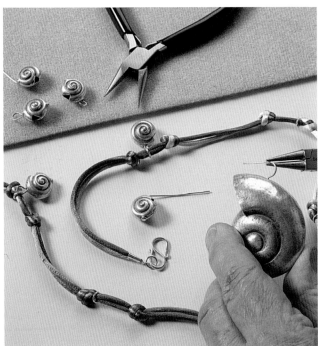

4. Push the large end pin through the snail, using the small silver bead as a stop if the hole in the snail is too large. Bend the end pin at a right angle at the top, then use the round-nosed pliers to make a small loop. Cut off the excess and close around the jump ring that you previously threaded around the cord. Attach the smaller snail charms in the same way using the smaller end pins.

Variation (*below*) This beautiful butterfly and silver leaf necklace is very much in the same style as the snail pendant. The leaves and central butterfly have been attached to a silver chain, with a woven rayon rainbow ribbon threaded through the jump rings. Indian silver charms and beads are available from specialist suppliers, although they can often be found in antique and flea markets too. Silver is usually sold by the weight.

Floating rainbow pearl disk necklace

This charming, elegant necklace is really worth making. The method is simple and really only consists of knotting the blue-toned mother-of-pearl disks onto five strands of blue silk thread. The necklace hangs in a pleasing and uniform way as the silk thread has some weight to it. Choose disks that have a hole punched close to the outer edge, rather than in the center. This necklace also needs to be stored suspended to prevent it tangling.

Technique:
TYING DISCS TO SILK THREAD

Level of difficulty:
EASY BUT VERY FIDDLY, NEEDS PATIENCE

Estimated making time:
1 1/2 HOURS

you will need

Pale blue silk cord, in medium thickness

50 mother of pearl discs, 3/4 in. (2cm) in diameter with a hole near the edge

2 round pale blue glass beads, approximately 1/4 in. (5mm) in diameter but with a large hole

2 silver box calottes

2 split rings. 1/4 in. (5mm) in diameter

1 lobster clasp with attached ring

Round-nosed pliers

Chain-nosed pliers

Scissors

1. Cut the silk cord into five 24in. (60cm) lengths. Starting approximately 2 3/4 in. (7cm) from one end, thread the first disk onto one of the lengths and tie a single knot to hold it in place.

2. Continue tying more discs to the cord, leaving a space of 1¹/₄–1¹/₂in. (3–4cm) between them until you have 12 disks on the cord.

3. Thread the second length of cord with 11 discs in exactly the same manner. Thread the third and fourth cords with 10 disks, and the fifth with 9 disks. Adjust the spacing, if necessary, so that all the cords have roughly 2³/₄in/ (7cm) spare at the end. Gather the ends together into two bundles and thread each bundle through a blue bead, then tie each bundle together in a knot at the very end.

4. Put the knotted silk into the box calotte and press in place with the round-nosed pliers. Press the calotte closed with the chain-nosed pliers. Attach the two split rings to the rings on the end of the calottes and attach the lobster clasp to one end.

Variation These dyed mother-of-pearl discs appear to be floating because nylon monofilament has been used to tie each one in place along the line. This is a very simple project that requires a certain amount of patience, but the result will be well worth the effort. Here three rows of discs have been joined together through a clam-shell calotte. This necklace needs to be stored carefully, as it may tangle if it is not suspended.

Mother-of-pearl shell pendant

This exquisite mother-of-pearl pendant necklace is the perfect piece of summer jewelry. The natural iridescence of the heart-shaped shell has been cleverly matched by adding an assortment of flower and leaf shapes cut from a similar shell, as well as silver and pink glass beads. The heart shape was already drilled with the small holes when purchased (the holes have been made with a crafters' drill), but it is possible to find shells with natural respiratory holes from which a similar fringe of beads may be suspended. Shells are some of the most beautiful specimens from the natural world and have been used for adornment and decoration throughout the ages. They are now widely available and are particularly adaptable for combining with other materials to make unique pieces of jewelry. Because they originate from the living world, we must always make sure they come from a sustainable source.

Technique:
**WORKING WITH LEATHER THONG,
ADDING SUSPENDED DECORATION**

Level of difficulty:
**SOME STAGES EASY, OTHER STAGES
MORE CHALLENGING**

Estimated making time:
2 HOURS

you will need

Heart-shaped mother-of-pearl shell, approximately $2^{1}/_{2}$in. (6cm) across with pre-drilled holes

Pink leather thong, approximately 22in. (55cm) long, $^{1}/_{16}$in. (1.5mm) thick

2 coils and loops, $^{1}/_{8}$in. (3mm) in diameter

Snake clasp, $^{3}/_{4}$in. (2cm) long

Jump ring, $^{1}/_{2}$in. (1cm) in diameter

Decorated pink glass lamp bead, $^{5}/_{8}$in. (1.5cm) long with a large hole

Silver bead, $^{3}/_{8}$in. (8mm) with a large hole

5 flattened silver beads, $^{3}/_{8}$in. (8mm) in diameter

2 pink glass beads, $^{1}/_{2}$in. (1cm) in diameter

2 pink glass beads, $^{3}/_{8}$in (8mm) in diameter

1 faceted glass bead, $^{5}/_{8}$in. (1.5cm) in diameter

4 mother-of-pearl leaves, $^{3}/_{4}$in. (2cm) long

1 mother-of-pearl flower, $1^{1}/_{4}$in. (3cm) in diameter

Tiger tail

Chain-nosed pliers

Scissors

5 silver crimp tubes

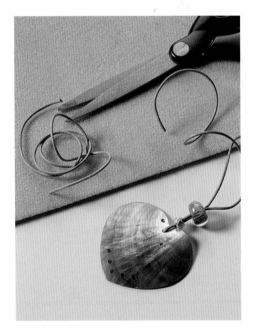

1. Thread the heart-shaped shell centrally onto the leather, bring the two ends together, and thread first through the silver bead with the large central hole. Next, thread on the large pink lamp bead and push them together next to the top of the heart.

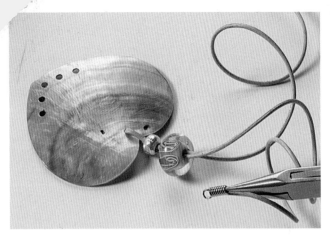

2. Push the end of the leather into the open end of the coil and loop, and use the chain-nosed pliers to press in the last coil to secure the leather. Attach the snake clasp to the ring at one end and the jump ring at the other end to fasten.

3. Cut five pieces of tiger tail approximately 10in. (25cm) long. Thread the mother-of-pearl flower centrally onto one of the lengths, fold in half, and thread the two ends through the faceted pink glass beads. Continue through a crimp tube and finally add a silver bead.

4. Take one end of the tiger tail through the central hole at the base of the heart and bring it back once more, through the silver bead, then through the crimp, and back through the glass bead.

5. Pull the tiger tail taut so there is no slack and press the crimp bead firmly with the chain-nosed pliers to secure. Cut off the excess tiger tail protruding from the glass and silver beads. To make sure it is hidden, push the beads toward the crimp tube before you cut. When the beads settle back, they will hide the tiger tail ends.

6. Continue in this manner, threading the other four dangles through the other four holes at the base of the heart, each one with a mother-of-pearl leaf followed by a smaller pink bead and a final silver bead. Use the smallest pink glass bead at the outer edge. Cut off the excess tiger tail to finish.

Variation Here glass beads and a ribbon thong have been chosen in colors to match a layered and lacquered bought shell pendant.

Variation This beautiful design is the height of elegance, with one perfect shell enhanced by a simple leather thong and a sprinkling of wood and silver beads.

suppliers

UK Suppliers

African Trade Beads
African beads and beading supplies
www.africantradebeads.com

Bead Addict
beads and beading supplies
www.beadaddict.co.uk

Bead Aura
3 Neals Yard
London WC2H 9DP
020 7836 3002
beads and beading supplies
beadaura@gmail.com
www.beadaura.co.uk

Bead Shop
21A Tower Street
London WC2 9NS
020 7240 0931
beads and beading supplies
www.beadshop.co.uk

Beadworks
online retailer of beads and beading supplies
www.beadworks.co.uk

Bijoux Beads
Elton House
2 Abbey Street
Bath BA1 1NN
01225 482024
beads and beading supplies
www.bijouxbeads.co.uk

Crystals
20 shops across southern England selling crystals and beading supplies
www.crystalshop.co.uk

London Bead Company
339 Kentish Town Road
London NW5 2TJ
0870 203 2323
beads and beading supplies
www.londonbeadco.co.uk

Spangles 4 Beads
beads and beading supplies
www.spangles4beads.co.uk

US Suppliers

Beadalon
205 Carter Drive
West Chester, PA 19382
866-423-2325
beading wire, stringing materials, tools
www.beadalon.com

The Beadin' Path
15 Main Street
Freeport, ME 04032
877-922-3237
vintage Lucite, unique beads/findings

Blue Moon Beads/Westrim Crafts
7855 Hayvenhurst Aveune
Van Nuys, CA 91406
800-377-6715
beads/findings
www.bluemoonbeads.com

Crystal Innovations/Pure Allure, Inc.
4005 Avenida De la Plata
Oceanside, CA 92056
800-536-6312
Swarovski crystal beads, crystal/metal sliders, clasps
www.pureallure.com

Euro Tool, Inc.
14101 Botts Road
Grandview, MO 64030
800-552-3131
tools, beading accessories
www.eurotool.com

Fire Mountain Gems and Beads
1 Fire Mountain Way
Grants Pass, OR 97526
800-355-2137
beads/findings, tools, stringing materials, kits
www.firemountaingems.com

Great Craft Works

133 West Gay Street
West Chester, PA 19380
888-811-5773
beads, tools, stringing materials
www.greatcraftworks.com

Halcraft, USA

30 West 24th Street
New York, NY 10010
212-376-1580
beads, tiny glass marbles
www.halcraft.com

Hirschberg Schutz and Co.

650 Liberty Avenue
Union, NJ 07083
908-810-1111
charms/embellishments

Lindstrom Tools

1440 West Taft Avenue
Orange, CA 92865
714-921-9950
beading tools
www.lindstromtools.com

Marvin Schwab, The Bead Warehouse

2740 Garfield Avenue
Silver Spring, MD 20910
301-565-0487
beads, gems, precious metal findings, stringing materials, tools
www.thebeadwarehouse.com

Natural Touch

P.O. Box 2713
Petaluma, CA 94953
707-781-0808
Indonesian resin beads
www.naturaltouchbeads.com

Offray Ribbon

Berwick Offray LLC
Bomboy Lane and Ninth Street
Berwick, PA 18603
800-237-9425
ribbon

Phoenix Beads, Jewelry and Parts

5 West 37th Street
New York, NY 10018
212-278-8688
imported glass, gemstone, pearl and crystal beads www.phoenixbeads.com

Paula Radke Dichroic Glass

P.O. Box 1088
Morro Bay, CA 93442
800-341-4945
dichroic beads
www.paularadke.com

Rings and Things

P.O. Box 450
Spokane, WA 99210
800-336-2156
beads, tools, findings, stringing materials
www.rings-things.com

Soft Flex Company

P.O. Box 80
Sonoma, CA 95476
707-938-3539
Soft Flex wire
www.softflexcompany.com

Swarovski North America Limited

1 Kenney Drive
Cranston, RI 02920
800-463-0849
Swarovski crystal beads, components

Thunderbird Supply

1907 West Historic Route 66
Gallup, NM 87301
800-545-7968
beads, findings, gemstones, tools, stringing materials
www.thunderbirdsupply.com

Toner Plastics

699 Silver Street
Agawam, MA 01001
413-798-1300
Fun Wire
www.tonerplastics.com

York Novelty

10 West 37th Street
New York, NY 10018
800-223-6676
Czech glass beads
www.yorkbeads.com

index

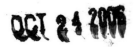